EX LIBRIS
PACE COLLEGE

41 PARK ROW, NEW YORK

TASTE in
Eighteenth Century France

*T*ASTE *in* *E*ighteenth *C*entury *F*rance

CRITICAL REFLECTIONS ON THE ORIGINS OF AESTHETICS

or

AN APOLOGY FOR AMATEURS

R. G. SAISSELIN

SYRACUSE UNIVERSITY PRESS

Copyright © 1965
by Syracuse University Press
Syracuse, New York

ALL RIGHTS RESERVED
First edition 1965

Library of Congress
Catalog Card 65-23460

Manufactured in the United States of America

BH
221.
F8S3

Preface

This book is not a history of eighteenth century aesthetics, although it was first conceived as a critique of such histories. In a first version the work was entitled "Critical Reflections on the Origins of Modern Aesthetics," a title modeled on that of the abbé Du Bos' *Réflexions critiques sur la poésie et sur la peinture* of 1719. Upon completion of the work, however, I had occasion to rethink the entire thesis in the light of other work done in the area of French eighteenth century painting and artistic thought and more specifically in connection with academic doctrines and the neoclassic style. I therefore ended with a book rather different from its original version.

The reader is asked not to expect any summaries of aesthetic doctrines arranged either chronologically or topically. Such studies exist and are readily available. Rather than produce another I have attempted to penetrate the eighteenth century mentality and set forth the reasons for eighteenth century thinking about the fine arts and taste. In short, why was taste not accepted as being either relative or subjective, even though philosophical thinking pointed in that direction?

I have concentrated on French writings on the arts because these are generally less well known in this country than are the more frequently studied German and British schools of aesthetics. Needless to say, I have not exhausted all the sources—partly because writings in this area are

v

numerous and often hard to find, but largely because it was not my intention to write an exhaustive study.

If the descriptive table of contents strikes the reader as odd in a book written in the twentieth century, he is asked to bear in mind that I have attempted to fit the form to the matter discussed.

Thanks are due to several persons who were of considerable help in the preparation of the first and final versions of this work. First, the patient, painstaking and charming secretaries of the Cleveland Museum of Art; their smiles, their willingness and readiness to turn out well-typed pages were of incalculable help. Second, thanks are also extended to that institution's director, who (despite his dislike of onionskin paper) took the time to read and comment upon these pages. Then too, thanks and appreciation must be given to the museum's able librarian, who always managed to find the books necessary to complete this study.

Rémy G. Saisselin

Paris, France
Spring, 1965

Contents

PART III: *Taste, Art, and Aesthetics*

Part I

The Fine Arts, Fable, and Reason

I

Introduction

It is generally admitted that modern aesthetic theory is a product of the eighteenth century. Credit for the new departure in speculations upon beauty and the arts is given either to the Germans, who with Baumgarten gave the new science or discipline a name; or to the British thinkers who with Addison gave an empirical direction to the new interest in beauty and aesthetic pleasure, while Shaftesbury oriented it to the examination of genius and intuitive aesthetics. Often the history of aesthetics in the eighteenth century, when not conceived in terms of a history of taste, or as studies of the sublime, beauty, or the picturesque, is written as a series of philosophical problems eventually resolved by Kant. Cassirer describes this history as follows in his work on eighteenth century thought:

The controversy over the definition and relative order of the various basic concepts, in which eighteenth century aesthetics was engaged, reflects the universal tendency in all its phases. Whether it is the dispute between reason and imagination, the conflict between genius and the rules, the foundation of the sense of beauty in feeling or a certain form of knowledge: in all these syntheses the same fundamental problem recurs. It is as if logic and aesthetics, as if pure knowledge and artistic intuition, had to be solved in terms of one another before either of them could find its own inner standard and understand itself in the light of its own relational complex.[1]

Aesthetics is thus seen as some immanent process leading logically and necessarily to Kant. As Paul Hazard writes in *La Pensée Européenne ou XVIII Siècle*: "Il fallait bien que la beauté, au lieu d'être objective, devînt subjective; au lieu d'être absolue relative; au lieu de dépendre de quelque notion ontologique, dépendit d'une modalité de notre être, puisque l'empirisme l'exigeait."[2] This logical process occurs independently of the thinkers involved, and so the history of aesthetics might be thought of as independent of men and of the arts.

"Individual thinkers participating in this movement," writes Cassirer, "are by no means aware from the start of the goal towards which they are steering; and in the clash of various tendencies a really consistent line of reasoning, a conscious orientation to a definitely conceived fundamental problem is nowhere to be observed." (277) Yet by the end of the century there had evolved a new form of philosophical aesthetics, and "all those trends, which considered in themselves might resemble bypaths of eighteenth century aesthetics, contributed indirectly to the appearance and the final attainment and determination of this form." (*Ibid.*)

One might suspect, in the face of such statements, that history is being read backwards, that a certain unity and logic are imposed on what Gibbon and Voltaire, who were historians, more accurately described as the crimes, follies, and misfortunes of mankind. At the same time we may also suppose that some of the difficulties in the writing of a history of aesthetics are due to the complexity and confusion of the subject itself. There is also the simple fact that the history of aesthetics has been written by philosophers rather than historians. Thus one proceeds like Kant, for whom the question of aesthetics was primarily philosophical, rather than a concern with the arts: "Die Kantische Ästhetik ist eine Antwort auf philosophische Fragen und nicht die Frucht eines Interesses für die Schönheit und die Kunst."[3] Following this line, problems appear where eighteenth century thinkers, poets, and artists saw none, and the history of aesthetics can be written quite independently of the knowledge of the arts and the social milieu of the period. This can be done because several straw men contributed to the history of aesthetics without realizing they were doing it, so that the history of aesthetics risks becoming that of innumerable *esthéticiens malgré eux*. The next step is to find the straw men; quite often people who wrote on taste, poetry, beauty, the sublime, became aestheticians. It is practical to divide these into two groups according to their approaches, and so to distinguish, in the eighteenth century, between philosophical aesthetics, largely German, and psychological and empirical aesthetics, largely British.

The French come out rather badly in the history of eighteenth century aesthetics, even though Du Bos, Batteux, Father André, and Diderot are mentioned. The French *philosophes* have fallen into disrepute. They are considered liberals, journalists, propagandists, but not philosophers worthy of being considered as possible rivals of the classical British philosophers such as Locke and Hume. Indeed, the latter expressed the issue rather well in the Introduction to his *Treatise of Human Nature* when he wrote "that however other nations may rival us in poetry, and excel us in some other agreeable arts, the improvements in reason and philosophy can only be owing to a land of toleration and of liberty."

However that may be, it does not follow that there was little French writing on aesthetics in the eighteenth century, or that the only writers worth consulting are the straw men alluded to above. It is true that there were few systematic treatises of aesthetic theory written in eighteenth century France. Father André and the abbé Batteux have been mentioned. The former's *Essai sur le Beau* was well thought of by Diderot, but as the latter wrote in his *Recherches philosophiques sur l'origine et la nature du beau,* he did not elaborate on "l'origine des notions qui se trouvent en nous, de rapport, d'ordre, de symétrie; car du ton sublime dont il parle de ces notions, on ne sait s'il les croit acquises et factices, ou s'il les croit innées."[4] The abbé Batteux is not even discussed in Raymond Bayer's recently published *Histoire de l'Esthétique,* yet Batteux's systematic little book, *Les Beaux-Arts réduits à un seul principe* (1746) is a good summary of eighteenth century thinking on the arts.

Again Diderot criticizes Batteux in much the same way as he did Father André: "M. l'abbé Batteux rappelle tous les principes des beaux-arts à l'imitation de la belle nature; mais il ne nous apprend point ce que c'est que *la belle nature.*" (*Ibid.,* p. 406) The language of the abbé Batteux is very vague, but that is precisely its strength: *la belle nature* is not to be defined conceptually with philosophical rigor and precision, but artistically by painters or poets. Diderot's criticisms point to one of the essential differences between aesthetics as thought in Britain and Germany on the one hand, and as thought and practiced in France on the other. We can say that aesthetics from above and from below, to use a by now consecrated expression, is not the sole way of treating this subject; in the France of Louis XV, aesthetics, to use a term which, with reference to that period, can only be an anachronism, is inseparable from reflection upon the fine arts as men knew them then, the social milieu, and the sense of history and values of civilization then current. In short, there is the aesthetics of the philosophers, which is distinguished by its own language, and proceeds from certain philosophical concepts and problems; and there is the way of thinking of the poets, painters, amateurs, *curieux*, and gentlemen who did not use philosophical language to discuss their tastes and the arts, but had recourse to the cultivated language of their times. If we fix our attention on the writings of these people we shall see that taste is much more complex than philosophers concerned with problems of cognition are likely to be aware of, and that thought upon the arts and taste cannot be isolated from the historical context without some violence to its understanding. It will then become necessary to reexamine some of the basic assumptions on which the history of eighteenth century aesthetics has been written.

These are, briefly repeated, that in history the arts, philosophy, and science are somehow linked and that consequently changes in philosophical and scientific thought engender changes in taste, criticism, and eventually in the arts. In short, one postulates a unity of thought and a logic of thought moved by some prime mover. Thus Cassirer can write:

As Kant saw in Rousseau the Newton of the moral world, eighteenth century aesthetics called for a Newton of art. And this demand no longer seemed incongruous after Boileau had been recognized as the "law-giver of Parnassus." His work seemed finally to elevate aesthetics to the rank of an exact science in that it introduced in the place of merely abstract postulates concrete application and special investigation. The parallelism of the arts and sciences, which is one of the fundamental theses of French classicism, now appeared to have been explained on the grounds of the common derivation of the arts and sciences from the absolutely homogeneous and sovereign power of "reason." This power knows no compromise and tolerates no qualification. (*Ibid.,* p. 280)

The history of aesthetics as treated by Cassirer is that of a progress, dialectical in nature, from Boileau to Kant. In fact, however, this constitutes no progress but merely a change of language and also, one is tempted to say, a confusion of languages based on a misreading of Boileau and a complete misunderstanding of that elusive phenomenon called French classicism, wrongly associated by some with Descartes. This confusion occurs because both Descartes and Boileau appeal to "reason," but the poet's "reason" is not that of the philosopher. Thus Cassirer may again write of Boileau that "in his *Poetic Art* he attempts to arrive at a general theory of the genres of poetry, just as the geometer attempts to arrive at a general theory of curves." (p. 289) The history of aesthetics thus parallels that of philosophy and science: "The inner transition by which the domination of classical theory in the realm of aesthetics is broken corresponds exactly from the point of view of method with the change which takes place in the theory of natural science between Descartes and Newton." (p. 297) In point of historical fact, however, these parallels are but figments of the philosophical imagination, constructions of the mind, and the inner transition which broke the classical dominance, assuming there ever was such a thing, might be something much more humble than it would seem from the writings of philosophers.

It seems obvious that one of the difficulties besetting Cassirer was French classicism; some elucidation of this is necessary before we can hope to make some progress in eighteenth century aesthetics. What is it? Rather than try to say what it is it might be wise to begin by stating what it is not: it is not academicism, it is not the "rules," it is not Boileau's *Art poétique*, and it is most certainly not Cartesianism in the arts. It is a psychology of art working, in the seventeenth century, within conventions called rules: distinction of genres, imitation of the ancients and of nature, the rule of the three unities of time, place and action for the theater, the practice of observing decorum and the rule of verisimilitude, and a hierarchy of motifs or genres. These distinctions were not imposed by Cartesian reasoning but by thought proper to the arts themselves and the word most apt to express it is *propriety*. Each genre has its own limits and potential, and the poet or painter observed its "rules" (an ambiguous term) for better artistic effect. These rules, we must stress, were not extensions of Cartesian thought and did not drastically limit the liberty of the poet or painter, because it was generally known they were not reversible. As Fontenelle wrote:

> Les églogues ont précédé les réflexions: j'ai composé, et puis j'ai pensé; et, à la honte de la raison, c'est ce qui arrive le plus communément. Ainsi je ne serai pas surpris si l'on trouve que je n'ai pas suivi mes propres règles, je ne les savais pas bien encore quand j'ai écrit: de plus, il est bien plus aisé de faire des règles, que de les suivre; et il est établi par l'usage que l'un n'oblige point à l'autre."[5]

Now it is quite true that in the first half of the century, Corneille was continually plagued by pedantic critics, and the difference between the philosopher and the artist, who both think on the arts, was already clear in the seventeenth century. Corneille knew just as well as Fontenelle that the rules were one thing and that to write a play was another, and he explained why in a telling manner, after repeating, just as everyone else would do for more than a century, that there were rules, but:

> Il faut donc savoir quelles sont ces règles; mais notre malheur est qu'Aristote, et Horace après lui, en ont écrit assez obscurément pour avoir besoin d'interprètes, et que ceux qui leur en ont voulu servir jusques ici ne les ont souvent expliqués qu'en grammairiens ou en philosophes. Comme ils avaient plus d'étude et de spéculation que d'expérience du théâtre, leur lecture nous peut rendre plus doctes, mais non pas nous donner beaucoup de lumières fort sûres pour y réussir.[6]

It is admirably put: the rules can be discussed, disputed, interpreted, refuted; but they can hardly be of service to the practicing man of letters or painter. They did for about two generations bother playwrights and poets because they were continually subject to the attacks of pedants. The important point to note about the seventeenth century is not so much the disputes and the papers written *pro* and *contra,* but how the whole question was resolved. There was nothing philosophically necessary about it at all; this "inner transition" has little to do with the transition from Descartes to Newton. The breakdown of the classical rules never occurred; writers simply ceased to discuss the matter, because of the risk of being ridiculous, since some poets who wrote on the rules and composed according to their principles had become objects of satire.

Had Chapelain kept to poetics and literary theory and not attempted to write an epic, he might have survived as an erudite of some merit rather than as Boileau's object of mockery. It would also have helped aesthetic theories if good plays had not been written in supposed violation of the rules. And it would have helped even more if jealous authors and critics had not aroused men like Molière and Boileau by wanting to demonstrate with the help of the discursive reason based upon Aristotle and Horace that obviously successful plays were, from the point of view of the rules, unsuccessful.

It turned out to be a mistake to criticize the *Ecole des femmes* because Molière ridiculed the critics, pedants and prudes, in his *Critique de l'école des Femmes*. This incident and this play alone should suffice to point out that nothing is more disastrous for some aesthetic theory or criticism than (1) works which succeed in spite of such theory and pass the test of time, (2) intelligent and witty practicing poets or painters, and (3) a history of the arts tied to simple human *tracasseries* rather than the immanent processes of reason working itself out in a logical or rational order.

Molière was in difficulties, as far as this play was concerned, with two types of critics: the *précieuses* and the *beau monde* who attacked his play on hearsay and because it was fashionable to do so; and the pedants who demonstrated on the basis of authority that his play was *irregular,* that is, not according to the rules. To counter these critics Molière used satire, ridicule, flattery, and appeals to generosity as well as some suggestions as to how to appreciate plays. Two types of people had to be removed as judges of the arts: prudes and experts. Someone else had to be found as a competent judge; Molière was in search of an audience, a public which would accept the

game of art. He succeeded in creating such a public because he enjoyed the protection of the king, and having
such a public, the emphasis on the rules was shifted to
something else. Molière asked through one of his characters whether the supreme rule of all were not to please
the audience and whether a play which had reached this
end had not followed the proper way to it. Obviously this
was hardly a philosophical argument or a good aesthetic
principle. But it was buttressed by the unfortunate fact
that a great many gentlemen who continually talked of
rules and apparently knew them better than others, always
seemed to write poor comedies. The conclusion was that
there must be something wrong with the rules:

> Si les pièces qui selon les règles ne plaisent pas, et que
> celles qui plaisent ne soient pas selon les règles, il fau-
> drait de nécessité que les règles eussent été mal faites.
> Moquons-nous donc de cette chicane où ils veulent assu-
> jéttir le goût du public, et ne consultons dans une
> comédie que les effets qu'elle fait sur nous. Laissons-
> nous aller de bonne foi aux choses qui nous prennent
> par les entrailles, et ne cherchons point de raisonnement
> pour nous empêcher d'avoir du plaisir.

This seems to point to something quite important: certain
attitudes, associated with certain audiences, are incompatible with artistic pleasure. Further, we note an important
shift of attention from rules to the pleasure of the spectator. Finally, it is not necessary to posit the triumph of
sensationalist philosophy, or some inner necessity, for this.
It is true that Molière read Gassendi, who rehabilitated
Epicurus, but it does not follow that he wrote as a hedonist aesthetician. He was a playwright pleading for and
with an audience, for as the dancing master in *Le Bour-
geois Gentilhomme* put it: "Il y a plaisir . . . à travailler

pour des personnes qui soient capables de sentir les déli-
catesses d'un art, qui sachent faire un doux accueil aux
beautés d'un ouvrage, et, par de chatouillantes approba-
tions, vous régaler de votre travail." It was precisely an
audience capable of such discernment which ushered in an
age of taste, *in which the articulate audience is no longer
primarily composed of pedantic critics, but gentlemen-
amateurs.* The change which occurred might be formulated thus: it was no longer permissible to be boring. As
Boileau wrote:

> Que vous ont fait Perrin, Bardin, Pradon, Hainaut,
> Colletet, Pelletin, Titreville, Quinault,
> Dont les noms en cent lieux, placés comme en leurs
>   niches,
> Vont de vos vers malins remplir les hémistiches?
> Ce qu'ils font vous ennuie. O le plaisant détour!
> Ils ont bien ennuyé le roi, toute la cour . . .[7]

Boileau was not the legislator of Parnassus even though
he was later called that. His importance lies precisely in
this formation of a class of readers who would no longer
put up with being bored. His *Art poétique* is not an
attempt at a general theory of genres, nor does it proceed
from the *esprit géométrique*. It is a treatise of poetics
addressed to the nonprofessional public; it is not a new
formulation of genres, but a restatement, in elegant and
clear language, of what poets and pedants had been saying ever since the 1620's. It was, further, an introduction
to the models of good poetry and writing, and as such laid
the foundation for a standard of taste and judgment based
on comparison. And, far from being a series of precepts
on how to write poetry in opposition to genius, it in fact
supposed genius to begin with; the very first verses read:

C'est en vain qu'au Parnasse un téméraire auteur
Pense de l'art des vers atteindre la hauteur:
S'il ne sent point du ciel l'influence secrète,
Si son astre en naissant ne l'a formé poète,
Dans son génie étroit il est toujours captif.

Boileau speaks no differently than Poussin, who in a letter of 1665 to Monsieur de Chambray speaks of the *rameau d'or de Virgile que nul ne peut trouver ni cueillir s'il n'est conduit par la fatalité,* for which there is no substitute. In short, long before Kant, it was known that some things can be taught, not essential as far as great art is concerned, and some which cannot be taught but which are the *je ne sais quoi* of true beauty.

With this term we have stumbled upon the crux of the matter concerning not only classicism, but also, perhaps, eighteenth century aesthetics in general; so that far from being the story of the logical resolution of philosophical problems, the history of eighteenth century aesthetics is perhaps only the story of the follies and misfortunes of philosophers attempting to define the *je ne sais quoi.*

There flourishes today in the British Isles a school of philosophy which would have it that most philosophical problems are the result of linguistic difficulties, ambiguities, or confusions. It may be that aesthetic problems could also be dissolved if language were clearer. And it could be that aesthetics as a separate branch of philosophy or as an autonomous science or discipline might disappear along with the linguistic difficulties. Pascal, long before Wittgenstein, made some remarks upon the difficulties involved when beauty and the arts are discussed:

Comme on dit beauté poétique on devrait aussi dire beauté géométrique, et beauté médicinale; mais on ne le dit pas: et la raison en est qu'on sait bien quel est l'objet de la géométrie, et qu'il consiste en preuves, et quel est l'objet de la médecine, et qu'il consiste en la guérison; mais on ne sait pas en quoi consiste l'agrément, qui est l'objet de la poésie. On ne sait ce que c'est que ce modèle naturel qu'il faut imiter. (*Pensées,* n. 133)

What Pascal does not say is that, in spite of this lack of knowledge or definitions, beauty and art do nevertheless exist, and poets and painters continue to produce poetic and artistic beauties. Aesthetics as a branch of philosophy became a potential when one grew aware of this ignorance; and the science of aesthetics became an actuality when attempts were made to define and probe this *je ne sais quoi* by searching for the origins of our notions of beauty. Pascal writing the above fragment may have thought as a philosopher and as a potential aesthetician. But when he wrote, long before Du Bos and Kant, that "Tout notre raisonnement se réduit à céder au sentiment," he had in a sense gone beyond aesthetics as it was to be understood among the Scots, English, and Germans of the eighteenth century. French aesthetics, if we may speak of it in those terms, kept to Pascal's sentiment; and Valéry's statement to the effect that "L'Esthétique des métaphysiciens exigeait que l'on séparât le Beau des belles choses"[8] aptly describes the course of eighteenth century aesthetics. The merit of the language of the classical period of France was that it was formed in rapport to the arts. It was this that gave an abstract, lucid, analytical, and psychological language, highly restricted in vocabulary but consequently rich in nuances, what the philosophers call referents.

In a sense we can even argue that it is precisely the vagueness of the terms beauty, poetry, imitation, decorum, *agréments,* and others which gave the poets and painters the freedom necessary for the creation of their works. There was, in short, no Winckelmann or Mengs to define beauty universally, precisely (and thus deadeningly). The *Conférences* of the *Académie Royale de Peinture* deceived no one: they talked one way and painted another. One professed a belief in universal standards of beauty, taught an official doctrine, probably little understood by Colbert, but bought what one wanted.[9] Thus it was known and accepted that tastes varied because the works of painters varied: "Les goûts des amateurs de la peinture ne sont pas moins différents que ceux des peintres," wrote Poussin, "et cette différence des goûts est la cause de la diversité qui se trouve dans les travaux des uns et dans les jugements des autres."[10] This variability and diversity did not seem to bother Poussin, Félibien, Roger de Piles, or Du Bos. But we may suppose that aesthetics as we have come to know it arose from an impatience with such variation and its corollary, the *je ne sais quoi*: the variations had to be explained because beauty was thought of in universal terms while individual works varied. Philosophers attempted to adapt a language suited either to metaphysical speculation or science to solve the seemingly inherent contradiction of the infinite variability of tastes. Poets and painters wrote and painted much as they had before, gentlemen and ladies took pleasure in the arts irrespective of what philosophers wrote, and Voltaire poked fun at the latter and thundered at the growing bad taste, due perhaps to a philosophical confusion we might call the naturalistic fallacy.

II

Of *Ancients and Moderns*

By historical accident, taste as the ultimate criterion for judging the fine arts first appeared in the midst of the scientific revolution of the *Grand Siècle*.

Molière and Boileau had no sooner defeated the pedantic critics than they were threatened by opponents much more formidable than the last of the Renaissance scholars. The fund of motifs on which poetry and painting had lived for so long was about to be dismissed as fable, illusion, and prejudice. Saint-Evremond, a French exile living in London in the latter half of the seventeenth century, pointed to the dilemma of poets and painters in a world of science as follows:

La vérité n'était pas du goût des premiers siècles; un mensonge utile, une fausseté heureuse, faisait l'intérêt des imposteurs, et le plaisir des crédules. C'était le secret des grands et des sages pour gouverner les peuples et les simples.

Le génie de notre siècle est tout opposé à cet esprit de fables et de faux mystères. Nous aimons les vérités déclarées: le bon sens prévaut aux illusions de la fantaisie! rien ne nous contente aujourd'hui que la solidité et la raison. Ajoutez à ce changement du goût, celui de la connaissance. Nous envisageons la nature autrement que les anciens ne l'ont regardée. Les cieux, cette de-

15

meure éternelle de tant de divinités, ne sont plus qu'un espace immense et fluide. Le même soleil nous luit encore; mais nous lui donnons un autre cours: au lieu de s'aller coucher dans la mer, il va éclairer un autre monde. La terre immobile autrefois, dans l'opinion des hommes, tourne aujourd'hui dans la nôtre, et rien n'est égal à la rapidité de son mouvement. Tout est changé; les dieux, la nature, la politique, les moeurs, le goût, les manières. Tant de changements n'en produiraient-ils point dans nos ouvrages? (*Oeuvres,* 1725, IV, 281-82)

The famous Quarrel of the Ancients and the Moderns grew out of this new world, and with this battle the liberties won by art over pedantry were also established vis-à-vis the new rationalists, and clarity of thought was extended even to the consideration of the arts.

The questions implied, but not clearly discerned, in the Quarrel were the following: (1) What is the relation of pleasure taken in works of the imagination to the rules of art? (2) What is the relation of works of the imagination to progress in the exact sciences? (3) What is the relation of the flourishing of the arts to society and history? These questions were never posed in this manner. The battle of the books began as a dispute among pedants, with passions raised on both sides, and the issues were never clearly formulated until Fontenelle and Du Bos intervened. And once the issues were well discerned, the answers came easily. It is of interest to note that the solution came not from pedants or scholars, but from amateurs of the sciences and the arts.[11]

It was the end of fables. A question of truth and of verisimilitude was involved. Suppose you wish to write a Christian epic, for after all, the modern world deserves its Christian epic; should you have recourse to pagan ornaments, metaphors, similes, allusions, figures? Is there not a contradiction between Christian subject-matter and forms drawn from a pagan world? Is art compatible with religious truth? Is Christian truth to be sacrificed to embellishments drawn from classical antiquity?

The confusion of the sacred and the profane, inherited from the Italian Renaissance, and which had apparently hardly bothered the Italians, no longer escaped the scrutiny of savants aware of the requirements of clear and distinct ideas. They were not alone in noting a certain contradiction inherent in the values and art of the *Grand Siècle*. The moralists noted, for example, an opposition between the idea of the gentleman, or *honnête homme*, and the requirements of the Christian life. And so another type of model was formed, the *homme de bien* who combined both Christian values and worldly manners if not a worldly spirit. It is easy to see why Molière could have run into difficulties. It was the time of the Compagnie du Saint Sacrement which had attempted to ban *Tartuffe*. Before the fine arts could hope to flourish in peace, the Tartuffes would have to be defeated.

But the poet was caught not only between the pedants and the pious. There was also danger from Cartesianism. Not from Descartes, who had known full well that the arts were the work of genius and not to be confused with inquiries into truth or ways to ultimate truth: "J'estimais fort l'éloquence, et j'étais amoureux de la poésie; mais je pensais que l'une et l'autre étaient des dons de l'esprit plutôt que des fruits de l'étude." (*Discours de la Méthode*, I) But the Cartesian philosophy could provide weapons to critics which might be dangerous. Cartesian doubt and method dismiss the past and totally undermine the classical doctrine of the imitation of the ancients. Cartesianism, in short, implied progress, or at least its possibility, so that long before the 1960's, even before Baudelaire's day, one could, in the seventeenth century, be "modern."

This could mean three things: one could be Christian and in the name of Christian truth discard the pagan past and, as a poet, attempt to write Christian, modern poetry; or one could be a Cartesian (and still be a Christian), and also argue for an art that would be modern and rational, rather than filled with fables and errors. It is here that Saint-Evremond's remarks on the universe are telling. There was, however, a third current of thought much more amenable to the arts than either Cartesianism or the Christianity of the day: Epicureanism, a current of thought more skeptical and much more worldly than the others, one which did not reject the past and did not believe in new starts.

The success of Galileo and Descartes and the new sciences in general had brought forth the idea that the moderns were the superiors of the ancients so that paradoxically the present was older than the past. The ancients, we often forget, might better be called the young. This view, expressed as early as 1669 in La Mothe le Vayer's *Mémorial de quelques conférences,* did not logically imply the dismissal of the past, but this step was soon taken.[12] Such thinking was tied to the praise of Louis XIV, who was compared to Augustus and lauded as the protector of arts and letters.

When a triumphal arch had to be erected a serious question arose: should the inscription be in Latin or French? The merits of both languages were hotly debated. To paraphrase Voltaire (who opined that behind every revolution there was a question of money), behind this and many other literary-scholarly quarrels there was a question of vanity; in this case there was also national pride. To praise Louis and his time was profitable. Writers and artists began to make comparisons between antiquity and the present; parallels between past and present were drawn and in the process philosophy, science, and the arts were confused. A progress, discernible in the exact sciences, was by some assumed also to hold good for the arts. In order to clear up the confusion, recourse was made to the Jesuitical use of distinctions. The Quarrel thus taught some how to think critically about the arts, and in the process of the dispute thinkers acquired a certain distance which made for better perception. Thus, it was the exigency of clarity associated with Descartes which in the end served to draw the distinctions which were to mark off the limits between the exact sciences, the fine arts, and philosophy.

The Quarrel might have lasted longer than it did had not its underlying assumptions been rationally examined. The whole affair could be satirized as Swift did in the *Battle of the Books,* resolving little thereby; but the whole question could also be shifted onto a new basis, as Fontenelle did when he examined the matter critically in his *Digressions sur les Anciens et les Modernes* (1688). The question of the preeminence of the ancients and the excellence of the moderns was stated in terms of a paradox: "Toute la question de la prééminence entre les anciens et les modernes étant une fois bien entendue, se réduit à savoir si les arbres qui étaient autrefois dans nos compagnes étaient plus grands que ceux d'aujourd'hui."

From a question debated rhetorically the Quarrel became a philosophical one and the issue was examined impersonally or disinterestedly. A constant was posed, for the question came to mean: did Plato, Demosthenes, or Homer have more wit or mind than their modern counterparts? Those who maintain that the ancients invented all the forms, perfected all the arts, and cannot be surpassed, assume precisely this: their nature was of a better quality than that of the moderns. This is erroneous: human nature is constant. But if so, what can explain the differences discernible in the works of ancients and moderns? Is it a question of climate, as some suppose? Hardly, for there is not enough difference between the climates of Greece, Rome, and France to change the inhabitants in any significant degree: "Nous voilà donc tous parfaitement égaux, anciens et modernes, Grecs, Latins, Français." Differences cannot be explained in terms of the nature of man or of a falling away from a golden age with its complementary better nature; but human institutions and history might supply the answer.

Fontenelle describes his approach as follows: "J'ai cru que le plus court était de consulter un peu sur tout ceci la physique, qui a le secret d'abréger bien des contestations que la rhétorique rend infinies." This may very well be taken as a turning point in the history of criticism and could be considered the beginning of modern criticism insofar as we understand the latter to be objective, disinterested, and not reasoned according to rules, authorities, or passions. From certain concepts about the ancients, the question was shifted to one of perception, and Fontenelle did for criticism what Descartes had done for philosophy.

The ancients were not physically or mentally the superiors of the moderns; if they invented most of the art forms known, it was simply because they were first in time. The moderns in their place probably would have done the same. But this is not to detract from their merit, for it does not follow that the moderns are their superiors, or even their equals, but merely that they have been able to profit from the mistakes, trials, and failures of the former. In a sense the moderns are in a situation less difficult than the ancients. The supposed superiority of the moderns is thus attributable merely to a process of trial and error. They may add to what the ancients did, but not always, and not in all fields of endeavor: "Afin que les modernes puissent toujours enchérir sur les anciens, il faut que les choses soient d'une espèce à le permettre." It is at this point that Fontenelle drew an important distinction between art and science, or between works of the imagination and those of the exact sciences:

L'éloquence et la poésie ne demandent qu'un certain nombre de vues assez borné par rapport à d'autres arts, et elles dépendent principalement de la vivacité de l'imagination. Or les hommes peuvent avoir amassé en peu de siècles un petit nombre de vues; et la vivacité d'imagination n'a pas besoin d'une longue suite d'expériences, ni d'une grande quantité de règles, pour avoir toute la perfection dont elle est capable. Mais la physique, la médecine, les mathématiques, sont composées d'un nombre infini de vues, et dépendent de la justesse du raisonnement, qui se perfectionne toujours; il faut même souvent qu'elles soient aidées par des expériences que le hazard fait naître, et qu'il n'amène pas à point nommé. Il est évident que tout cela n'a point de fin, et que les dernier physiciens devront naturellement être les plus habiles. (III, 125)

The distinction drawn here seems to be the one Valéry had in mind two centuries later when in his dialogue, *Eupalinos, ou l'architecte,* he distinguished between *le connaître et le construire.* Science is the pursuit of knowledge and knowledge, once acquired, is cumulative; but art is another matter, it is construction and it is noncumulative. In science there is progress; in art there is something called *perfectionnement.* The arts are thus limited by man's imaginative capacity; a work in a given genre may be better than another and certain genres may be perfected and their possibilities exhausted. Thus, thought Fontenelle, Demosthenes and Cicero can hardly be improved on in the realm of eloquence, Titus Livius can hardly be surpassed in history, and certain verses of Virgil can never be equaled. However, plots, characters, or situations may change, and new ones may be invented, as the novel and the opera readily show. Furthermore, although the ancients seem to have attained perfection in certain genres, it does not follow that they are beyond criticism and that they are to be accepted unconditionally: "Il faut être capable de dire ou d'entendre dire, sans adoucissement, qu'il y a une impertinence dans Homère ou dans Pindare; il faut avoir la hardiesse de croire que des yeux mortels peuvent apercevoir des défauts dans ces grands génies."

Just as the poets and playwrights had to gain freedom from the constraint of the rules, based on authority, so the reader or spectator had to gain freedom of judgment, also thought of as freedom from some authority. In other words, it appears that freedom of mind, thought, and artistic judgment are inseparable. At the same time it appears that works of imagination are no longer to be the subject of passionate commitment and partisanship insofar as criticism is concerned; rather a certain distance between the judge and the work in question has been established. The man of taste, it would seem, is as free from the authority of ancient philosophers, as he is from that of the moderns, as free from the weight of the past as from the present, as free from the church fathers as from the modern pedantic critics. All this does not mean he was a libertine, but merely that he freely accepted certain social and religious conventions now seen to be just that.

The question remained: on what basis could one say that there were or were not impertinences in Homer or Pindar? Was such a pronouncement to be based purely on personal likes and dislikes? Was it to be purely gratuitous or could some convincing reasons be given for one's opinions concerning works of imagination? It is clear that just as Descartes had to learn to think critically, so in a sense one had to learn to read and judge critically in the fine arts. One had to find the type of thinking appropriate to the object.

Consider Homer. How should he be read? In Greek, to be sure; but if the reader knew no Greek and read a translation, the music of the poetry escaped him. Further, the early eighteenth century reader had to keep in mind that Homer did not live in times similar to those familiar to his reader. Thus argued Madame Dacier, a French scholar of the period famous for her translations of ancient authors, in her preface to her prose translation of the *Iliad* which appeared in 1711. La Motte-Houdar, a learned poet, answered with a verse translation of Homer. He knew no Greek, but since he wished to adapt Homer to the present, this lack of knowledge did not disturb him. He explained his intentions in his *Réflexions sur la critique* and showed himself to be a Descartes of poetry:

L'Iliade d'Homère que bien des gens connaissent plus par réputation que par elle-même, m'a paru mériter d'être mise en vers français, pour amuser la curiosité de ceux qui ne savent pas la langue originale. Pour cela j'interroge Homère; c'est-à-dire que je lis son ouvrage avec attention; et persuadé en le lisant que rien n'est parfait, et que les fautes sont inséparables de l'humanité, je suis en garde contre la prévention, afin de ne pas confondre les beautés et les fautes. Je crois sentir ensuite que les dieux et les héros, tels qu'ils sont dans le poème grec, ne seraient pas de notre goût; que beaucoup d'épisodes paraîtraient trop longs; que les harangues des combattants seraient jugées hors d'oeuvre, et que le bouclier d'Achille paraîtrait confus, et déraisonnablement merveilleux. Plus je médite ces sentiments, plus je m'y confirme; et après y avoir pensé autant que l'exige le respect qu'on doit au public, je me propose de changer, de retrancher, d'inventer même dans le besoin; de faire enfin selon ma portée, tout ce que j'imagine qu'Homère eût fait s'il avait eu affaire à mon siècle. (*Oeuvres,* 1754, III, 8-9)

La Motte's reasoning is delightfully revealing: he must, in order to perfect or polish Homer, assume that his society produces a better poetry and is generally more civilized than that of Homer. But he also shows the danger inherent in the arguments used by Molière to defend himself from his critics: if the first of all rules is to please, whom is one to please? Furthermore, La Motte has introduced into his literary endeavor a form of thinking alien to it: the idea of progress proper to the sciences has been used to correct Homer, who thereby loses his integrity and independence. La Motte questions the reputation of Homer much as Descartes did that of the philosophy of the Middle Ages and the ancients. Homer's reputation is merely something due to scholars and this can be demolished easily by reason. Authority no longer counts: "A la vue des premières expériences de la pesanteur de l'air, qu'a servi le long règne de l'horreur du vide?"

For all we know, Homer's reputation rests on mere fable and on the uncritical acceptance of authorities.

With La Motte, then, the quarrel between ancients and moderns broadened into one between poetry and physics, and the muses, saved for a short time from pedants and prudes, were about to fall victims to those who would reduce all artistic endeavor to a mere amusement or else would subject them to some universal rational Cartesian criticism.

III

A Digression on Poetry,
Science, and Time

It has always been difficult to be a poet, but it is quite likely that it may have seemed more difficult to be one in the early eighteenth century than ever before. If not caned for impertinence, poets ran the risk of ridicule. They appeared highly unreasonable. Montesquieu described them in his *Lettres persanes:* "Ce sont ici les poètes . . . , c'est-à-dire ces auteurs dont le métier est de mettre des entraves au bon sens et d'accabler la raison sous les agréments" (Letter 147).[13] Value was about to be put on reason, common sense, and clarity of thought; fancy, imagination, enthusiasm, and poets were to suffer in consequence. The question of the relation of science (as it was thought of) to poetry supposes a question of wide scope: some men in the early eighteenth century wondered whether poetry, as they knew it, was possible in a mechanistic universe. To us, coming as we do after romanticism, the question may seem to have been badly posed. But then, in the early eighteenth century writers had just learned how to pose such questions.

Saint-Evremond, as we have seen, considered the new intellectual climate of the second half of the seventeenth century unsuited to the world of poetic fable inherited from the past. Montesquieu later echoed this sentiment with reference to the notion of the sublime which had,

26

according to Boileau, who based himself on Longinus, been interpreted as "l'extraordinaire, le surprenant, et . . . le merveilleux dans le discours." The latter phrase, *dans le discours,* is worth noting; for the intellectual revolution of the *Grand Siècle* alluded to by Saint-Evremond, would precisely affect discourse and touch upon poetry by that way.

But the sublime was also foreign to the men of the eighteenth century. Many, fixing their attention upon the new cosmos revealed by mechanics, lost the feeling of the sublime. Montesquieu explained why:

> Mais ce qui achève de perdre le sublime parmi nous et nous empêche de frapper et d'être frappés, c'est cette nouvelle philosophie qui ne nous parle que de lois générales et nous ôte de l'esprit toutes les pensées particulières de la Divinité. Réduisant tout à la communication des mouvements, elle ne parle que d'entendement pur, d'idées claires, de raison, de principes, de conséquences. Cette philosophie, qui est descendue jusqu'à ce sexe qui ne semble être fait que pour l'admiration, diminue le goût que l'on a naturellement pour la poésie. (*Oeuvres*, I, 1019)

Now, as Mallarmé would one day tell Degas, you don't write poetry with ideas but with words. The early eighteenth century, because of the poetry it inherited and because of the rhetorical nature of the arts, was not yet aware of this but realized full well that it would be difficult to write poetry with clear and distinct ideas.

However, it would be too simple to assume that it was the new cosmos alone which made of the early eighteenth century what has been rightly called the *nadir of French poetry.* There was another cause involved, namely the ennui produced by a poetry which could be written with the use of stock images, themes, and a dictionary of rhymes. The motifs of the old poetry had been used too long to still touch and be of interest. Fontenelle points to this issue in his essay *Sur la poésie en générale:*

> Je lis une tempête décrite en très beaux vers: il n'y manque rien de tout ce qu'ont pu voir, de tout ce qu'ont pu ressentir ceux qui l'ont essuyée; mais il y manque Neptune en courroux avec son Trident. En bonne foi, m'aviserai-je de le regretter, ou aurais-je le tort de ne pas m'en aviser? Qu'eut-il fait là de plus que ce que j'ai vu? Je le défie de lever les eaux plus haut qu'elles ne l'ont été, de répandre plus d'horreur dans ce malheureux vaisseau, et ainsi de tout le reste; la réalité seule a tout épuisé. (*Oeuvres,* 1757, IV, 258-59)

Poetry suffered from too many well-known mythological allusions in a world disbelieving in fable. These allusions had become the mere ornaments or agreeable parts of poetry. The Cartesians of the day consequently, like the Miesians of today in architecture, meant to rid poetry of ornament and embellishments; an honest, sensible, and reasonable poetry was required. Reality was to suffice. The sky was being emptied of ancient divinities and the wind was no longer to be a zephyr, or thunder a bolt hurled by Zeus. The criticism which had questioned the fabulous past, and so taught to distinguish between fable and history, ran over into poetry and threatened its very existence. Consider, too, that poetry was surpassed, insofar as images and ornament were concerned, by painting. The situation of the poet and of poetry in the early eighteenth century thus appeared serious indeed.

Given the requirements of reason, clarity, and truth, given the superiority of images of sight to those of mind, what could remain of poetry? Indeed, one could even ask:

what is poetry? That such a question should have been put is indicative enough of the import of the intellectual revolution of the times: you do not ask such questions in periods of full artistic creativity. For La Motte-Houdar, *poète et cartésien mondain,* if we may so call him, poetry was what we today would call *functional:* something neutral, merely a form of discourse which could be used to any purpose. Committing the naturalistic fallacy, he saw no reason why Racine's tragedies should not be as good in prose as in verse. Poetry is a technique and one he did not think too much of: what mattered was that one please the public. As for inspiration and enthusiasm, the supposed wellsprings of poetry, it stood to reason they could find little place in a world more and more dominated by mechanism. In fact, enthusiasm and inspiration were more harmful than necessary. Asking himself what enthusiasm was, he answered: "Voilà donc précisément l'idée de l'Enthousiasme: c'est une chaleur d'imagination qu'on excite en soi, et à laquelle on s'abandonne; source de beautés et de défauts, selon qu'elle est aveugle ou éclairée. Mais c'est le plus souvent un beau nom qu'on donne à ce qui est le moins raisonable." (1754, I, 28) It was, in short, an overheated imagination, creator of fancies and illusions, and greatly in need of the cold shower of reason.

Fontenelle, La Motte's contemporary, thought no differently and associated enthusiasm with a form of instinct, what was most animal in man. To be sure, a work of imagination might charm us and show what the seventeenth century so well termed *un beau désordre,* but this was to be the effect of art, rather than of enthusiasm. Poetry ought not to be written under the effect of inspiration. Great and perfect works could only be the result of art, which must tame the fires of genius and inspiration.

Since poetry is written for a public of ladies and gentlemen, it should be clear; by this La Motte meant clarity of the self-evident type which made effort unnecessary for the reader, thence the use of method and organization: "Pour moi," he wrote in his *Discours sur la poésie en général et sur l'ode en particulier,* "je crois independament des exemples, qu'il faut de la méthode dans toutes sortes d'ouvrages." (I, 31) Given this requirement of method one can see why the Sublime should fare no better than enthusiasm. The Sublime was reduced to something rather mechanical. The attempt to define the Sublime in a rational manner is itself of note since, like the *je ne sais quoi,* it was something to move the soul, rather than to be defined.

Good analyst that he was, La Motte thought that definitions of the Sublime had not really been definitions at all, but merely examples: "Il me semble que jusqu'à présent on en a plûtot donné des exemples que des définitions. Il est néanmoins important d'en fixer l'idée; car les exemples ne sont que des moyens de comparaison, sujets à mille erreurs; au lieu que les définitions font juger des choses par un principe invariable, sans avoir recours à des analogies toujours très-imparfaites." (I, 35) Certainly La Motte ought to be the preferred poet of the present-day philosophical analysts and positivists. Long before Baumgarten he yearned, so to say, for an aesthetic which would provide invariable principles. How then does a Cartesian like La Motte define the Sublime? "Je crois que le Sublime n'est autre chose que le vrai et le nouveau réunis dans une grande idée, exprimés avec élégance et précision."

The difference between La Motte and Boileau is revealing, for in spite of what he says about examples, La Motte

has to have recourse to them, and he takes the one everyone seemed to use at the time, namely: *Dieu dit que la
lumière se fasse, et la lumière se fit*, or, more strongly in
English: *And God said: Let there be Light, and there was
Light*. For La Motte this thought, this great idea, is what
he calls *une vérité positive*. For La Motte the Sublime of
this sentence resided in the truth of the statement; for
Boileau, who used the same illustration, the Sublime lay
in the style, in the form of the statement. The difference
is that between a philosopher and an artist. The philosopher, like the theologian, is interested in the truth of a
proposition, but the literary critic Boileau, and the man
of taste of the eighteenth century, is interested in the form.
Let us note that La Motte's insistence on elegance and
precision are hardly likely to produce feelings of the
Sublime.

Fontenelle, also a Cartesian, was more penetrating than
La Motte, even though their views on poetry are very
similar. But his grasp of the problems seems more profound. He realized that the new mental universe would
require a new poetry: the old metaphors had become com-
monplaces to be used indifferently by good or bad poets.
The world of mythology inherited from the Greeks and
Romans, though vast, was now so well known as to force
banality into verse and poetry. As for inspiration, no one
believed in it anymore and poets could no longer claim to
be divinely inspired because they introduced mythology
into their poetry. "Ce qui a dû passer autrefois pour une
inspiration surnaturelle, n'est plus aujourd'hui qu'une
répétition dont tout le monde est capable." (IV, 262)
Fontenelle allowed, however, that if one did give up
mythology in poetry, one still might have recourse to what
he called semi-fabulous images, by which he meant ab-

stract ideas such as generosity, virtue, abundance, etc. These were the sort of subjects painters might treat in allegory.

However, what he recommended above all was a poetry to be constructed on the vision of the universe brought to light by modern science. This poetry was no longer to be made up of images of sight, old metaphors and mythological elements derived from the ancients, but of what he termed images of mind. Viewed in the context of the times the distinction is quite important. For we must recall that until this time poetry had been founded upon images of sight. It was this which gave meaning to the _ut pictura poesis_ of Horace. Fontenelle's distinction, had it been implemented, would have led to a poetry divorced from painting. Du Bos' considerations on poetry and painting were also governed by this notion of poetry and painting as being made up of images of sight. The reform in poetry, however, would only come in the later nineteenth century with the work of Mallarmé and the answer to Fontenelle is perhaps Paul Valéry. Fontenelle thought that poets should seek inspiration in metaphysical images and consider as possible motifs such notions as the general order of the universe, time, space, mind, divinity. He gave examples of this type of new poetry, but these do not strike one as particularly successful, or _moving_.

Needless to say, such a poetry would require a new type of poet: poet and philosopher became one, but it must be understood that philosophy was now to a great extent Cartesian, no longer Platonic. The poets, in short, ought to profit from the new philosophy; he thought it had already done wonders for poetry:

Il n'est pas douteux que le Philosophie n'ait acquis aujourd'hui quelques nouveaux degrés de perfection.

De là se répand une lumière qui ne se renferme pas dans la région philosophique, mais qui gagne de proche, et s'étend enfin sur tout l'empire des lettres. L'ordre, la clarté, la justesse, qui n'étaient pas autrefois des qualités trop communes chez les meilleurs auteurs, le sont aujourd'hui beaucoup davantage, et même chez les médiocres. Le changement en bien jusqu'à un certain point est assez sensible partout. La poésie se piquera-t-elle du glorieux privilège d'en être exempte?" (IV, 274-75)

There were those who, following this train of thought, assumed (long before Hegel) that poetry would eventually have to disappear and be replaced by philosophy. The abbé Trublet, biographer of Fontenelle, described the possibility: "Plus la raison se perfectionnera, plus le jugement sera préféré à l'imagination; et par conséquent moins les poètes seront goûtés. Les premiers écrivains, dit-on, ont été poètes. Je le crois bien; ils ne pouvaient guère être autre chose. Les derniers seront philosophes." Considering the rise of aesthetics, our criticism, and the state of poetry, the novel, and painting in our times, it appears that Trublet and Hegel were not far wrong—although, if they are right, perhaps not for the reasons they had in mind.

Not everyone was happy about this possibility in the eighteenth century. Voltaire and others complained of the empire which physics was beginning to assume over poetry. A bad poem by Chabanon put the matter as follows: poetry is dying because the scientific spirit is opposed to poetry; the latter comes from the heart, not the brain. As for analysis, it is a sure means of removing the arts from our lives. Fénelon, the Archbishop of Cambray, and apologist of *quiétisme,* also rose to the defense of poetry. He was indeed among the few men of the period to realize that poetry was something more than fable, technique, discourse, or a *difficulté vaincue* and the pleasure derived therefrom. Nor was it a mere society game. Poetry was something allied to religion, so that even the Bible could be read as poetry: "Toute l'Ecriture est pleine de poésie dans les endroits mêmes où l'on ne trouve aucune trace de versification."[14] The role of poetry in early society was consequently enormous and could hardly be dismissed as mere prejudice. Turning his attention to his own times he realized fully well the reasons for the sick estate of poetry, but he was no more able to prescribe an effective remedy than any other contemporary. Unlike Fontenelle, he did think that poetry must move the reader and transport him to a world of illusion. Poetry was tied to the dream of the Golden Age. He was also aware that one of the major difficulties facing the French poet resided in the nature of the French language. This chaste, clear, precise, and analytical language of a restricted social and intellectual milieu was hardly conducive to the creation of the *élans de coeur* necessary for poetic effect. His recommendation to have recourse to Latin neologisms could bear no fruit. Even Fénelon was too much of his time to see much hope for poetry.

There would indeed be no renewal of poetry for about two generations and the discussion between poetry and philosophy, or between the muses and the new exact sciences, would continue into the reign of Louis XV. Condillac took up the question in his *Traité de l'art d'écrire* and points succinctly to the reason poetry was almost impossible in the eighteenth century:

> Quand une fois la clarté et la précision font le caractère d'une langue, il n'est plus possible de bien écrire sans être clair et précis. C'est une loi à laquelle les poètes

mêmes sont forcés de se soumettre, s'ils veulent s'assurer de succès durables. Ils se tromperaient s'il s'en reposaient sur leur enthousiasme ou sur leur réputation. Il n'y a que la justesse des expressions qui puisse accréditer les tours qu'il leur est permis de hasarder; et, à cet égard, la poésie française est une des plus scrupuleuses.[15]

We note that by now the question of the relation of poetry and science has taken a new turn and that what the poet has to contend with is no longer whether he can or cannot use metaphors which are derived from a dead mythology and a world of fable. His problem has become one of dealing with a language conditioned by the requirements of clarity, a requirement also associated with the exact sciences. But further, he has to deal with a public whose taste has become more exacting and difficult to please. This consideration led Condillac to make an interesting remark: he thought that Greek poetry was meant to be read out loud and heard and so judged by sound, whereas French poetry was meant to be read and in a sense examined by the critical mind. It had become, perhaps since Father Bouhours' criticism, a poetry made for connoisseurs of the French language. The modern world thus turned out to be much more difficult for the poet than the one in which he had had fables at his disposal. Taste had become surer, more refined, and more acquainted with the arts: there was more matter to compare. Poets were constrained to please this public of connoisseurs with exactitude of image and correction of style. Condillac, as much as Montesquieu, or Gibbon remarking on it in his *Essai sur l'étude de la littérature,* realized that the world had been in a sense *depoetized,* but his attitude was quite different from that of a Montesquieu who still felt a nostalgia for antiquity and the innocence and simplicity associated with it. Condillac considers simply that the prejudices of the past have finally been vanquished. The world of poetry, by now associated with a distant past of fable and myth, has been lost. The new age cared no longer for the amiable illusions of poetry, but truths which, wrote Condillac, "ne se peignent pas avec la même facilité que les préjugés; elles n'ouvrent pas la même carrière à l'imagination; elles obligent à une précision plus scrupuleuse, et par conséquent il faut plus de génie pour être poète. M. de Voltaire est un modèle dans ce genre de poésie." (V, 487-88)

The same issue of poetry and the new truths was treated by d'Alembert in his *Dialogue entre la poésie et la philosophie.*[16] It turns out that truth is to be thought of in didactic-moral terms. Poetry complains to the effect that only useful reading obtains the approval of philosophy. Philosophy, being an able dialectician, readily overcomes the complaint of Poetry by the simple device of redefining the assertion: "Il est certain que les ouvrages qui joignent l'instruction à l'agrément, ont la première place auprès de moi; et ce même Horace, que je ne me lasserai point de vous citer, pensait aussi de même: souvenez-vous de l'*omne tulit punctum qui miscuit utile dulci.* Mais je ne proscris pas les poésies de pur agrément, pourvu qu'elles contiennent des beautés propres *à l'auteur,* et par conséquent *nouvelles;* je dirai, si vous voulez, en ce sens, *que la poésie même me déplaît quand elle ne m'apprend rien.*" The passage is quite remarkable. There is an ambiguity here which resides in the notion of utility. We may suspect that when d'Alembert used the term it meant something quite different from what it did in Antiquity. Let us further note that originality has been associated with the new, and one wonders whether it is still originality as Pope understood it, namely

What oft was thought, but ne'er so well expressed?

Considering the period in question we may suspect that more is involved. D'Alembert, like Fontenelle, calls for a new poetry; what he questioned was the whole rhetorical basis of the arts, for as he says—in answer to an objection that philosophers prefer thoughts to images—if images are the stuff of poetry, then eloquence and history and painting are also poetry, and many excellent verses contain no images. Verses are not remembered for their images, but because they express new and true ideas in a striking manner. With this remark, however, one finds oneself once more in the seventeenth century, for d'Alembert thought it was precisely this which distinguished the poets of the *Grand Siècle* from the more mediocre and less inventive ones of his own time. What he failed to see, or had forgotten, was that the poets of the seventeenth century had not created such poetry following a discussion of the nature of poetry, or its requirements in a new mental universe.

It may well be that the entire question was as ill-put as that between the ancients and the moderns. A new poetry could hardly come from a philosophical discussion. The *Grand Siècle* had known it was the work of genius. The generation of Fontenelle and Montesquieu had learned that genius could only work within certain historical contexts. The discussion of the nature of poetry in the eighteenth century shows that the context was then not propitious to poetic thought. The discussion would end only when a born poet would produce the new poetry in spite of all the arguments against poetry. For this one had to wait for André Chénier, who was inspired by a vision not of the new cosmos but, significantly, of the old human world of the antique. Another remote past still inspired the poet; the world of fable, criticized by reason, gave way to that of history. Poetry was saved by the sense of the past.

If reason relegated fable to an absurd or poetic past, if worldly taste could reduce poetry to a mere social game, how could poetry, and we might even say, how could the fine arts which, as Voltaire put it, all joined hands, survive in this new world of science?

Some distinctions might be drawn here. Certain aspects of Cartesian thought are not incompatible with the arts at all. For clarity of thought is not the enemy of artistic creation and work. The Cartesian notion of clear and distinct ideas is compatible with artistic thought; it insists upon perception. It is true that many books and articles about the influence of science upon the arts are produced in our day and in the eighteenth century such influence did exist and exerted itself upon prose. But the argument could be reversed and we could equally well write books and articles about the influence of the arts on science. And the seventeenth century might well be the subject of one of these. Thus architects and landscapists could be "classically clear," and in this very restricted sense Cartesian, and yet still use ornament; and a rococo interior, even though reasonably organized, need not be, because of this insistence on reason, the prototype of a Swedish or Danish interior.[17] Clearly it was poetry which suffered most from what is derived from the Cartesian *esprit de géométrie*. And it is this, rather than Descartes, who had something of the mystic in him and was himself a great artist of thought, which would endanger the fine arts. It might be called a variety of reductionism or what Etienne Gilson called linguistic imperialism, that is, imperialism of the discursive reason. The question thus might be re-phrased as follows: what could save poetry from con-ceptual thought? Or, what could save Homer from La Motte-Houdar?

Strangely enough it was the sense of historical change. The classical rules were a-historical and decorum regulated the relation between the spectator, in the present, and the play, painting, or poem representing an action of the past. The relation of past to present was thus par excellence artistic: it allowed the poet or painter the latitude needed for the creation of original works. The past was to be a model for inspiration, not for copying. Thus the Greeks or Romans of Corneille or Racine were not copies but motifs used for a contemporary theater and drama. One might say, then, that before the Quarrel of the Ancients and the Moderns, the seventeenth century did not have a sense of historical change. To be sure there was a past, but it was thought of as a present removed in time. This is probably why one could *imitate* the ancients not only in the making of works of art, but also in the making of the gentleman, that is, in the realm of mores. Imitation would then in this sense mean "re-thinking," "re-creation." The *honnête homme* as well as poet and painter imitated the ancients, even when one talked of imitating nature. The past was a fund of ideal types. In such a relation of present to past, the latter is made use of by the former. The past is kept alive by the present, and the past at the same time artistically informs the present. And so one may, in the present, continue the old comedy, continue the old tragedy. Louis XIV might, if he wished, play at being Augustus, and later Napoleon, with the help of Talma and David, could play at being Caesar.

The artistic relation of past and present could, however, be broken by Cartesian thought. Paradoxically it was the a-historical Cartesianism of the seventeenth century which ushered in a sense of historical change. The achievements not only of the new physics but also of the new literature (for science and letters were not thought of separately) made men aware that their times, and also their particular western European society, were different not only from other societies removed in time but also from others present but removed in space. Mores, times, and the arts were subject to change, and so too was the idea of beauty and taste. The work of Molière and Boileau which had transferred competence in the judging of works of imagination from the rules of the pedants to the taste of the *honnêtes gens* was about to be questioned. It became a commonplace of the eighteenth century to say that tastes varied historically and geographically. As Voltaire put it in his *Essay on Dramatic Poesy* (written in English, 1726), making a distinction between the exact sciences and the arts: "We may define metals, minerals, elements, animals, because their nature is ever the same; but almost all the works of man change as does the imagination which produced them. The customs, languages, and the taste of the closest neighbors differ." The rules ceased to be universally valid because of their historicity. The only rule to survive this historical relativism was, Voltaire thought, that an action be *one and simple, great, interesting, complete.* Evidently this rule could be used in any time and amounted to a mere observation of what it is that holds men's attention to certain works beyond historical time. The remainder—that is, the episodic, the marvelous, the plot even, the motifs, the conventional—belonged to historical time and certain places and climes and were generally called *local beauties* or *local color.* The great and complete action was universal, it was the general beauty of the work.

We have said that it was a commonplace of the eighteenth century to repeat that tastes varied. Yet no one would accept the logical consequences of this, probably on the good grounds that art is one thing and logic another but possibly also because of certain habits of mind and because taste was a subject of discourse, which in the eighteenth century tended to be universalizing. And so eighteenth century gentlemen, critics, artists, and poets continued to believe in a true and universal taste in spite of historical evidence to the contrary. The complete relativization of taste came only much later in the nineteenth century.

The lesson drawn from this impact of historical thought and change upon critics was that they ought to learn to read and see. Thus, for example, they distinguished between certain types of texts. Poetry is not read in the same way as a treatise in physics: "Pour juger des poètes," wrote Voltaire, "il faut savoir sentir, il faut être né avec quelques étincelles du feu qui anime ceux qu'on veut connaître; comme pour décider sur la musique ce n'est pas assez, ce n'est même rien de calculer en mathématicien la proportion des tons, il faut avoir de l'oreille et de l'âme."[18] But you also had to have a sense of historical time and change. As the abbé Du Bos, discussing this very problem, put it: "Nous devons nous transformer en ceux pour qui le poème fut écrit, si nous voulons juger sainement de ses images, de ses figures, et de ses sentiments."[19] The sense of historical change, then, taught some how to read, how to see, and how to judge of works of the imagination, and it was the personal delectation of such works, coupled with this historical sense, which combined to form a firmer taste than that of the generation of Molière and Boileau.

This new type of artistic judgment also saved works of imagination from complete historical relativism, as

well as rationalism. The works of the imagination were
distinguished from the exact sciences; but also, they were
lifted from the flux of time itself. Works of art, born of
history, became a-historical, while science was not accorded
this type of immortality. In the realm of the exact
sciences the achievements of the past were always subject
to doubt, question, reversal, replacement. We can make
table rase of certain systems of philosophy or science if
doing so will bring us supposedly closer to the desired end.
Here the past truly dies; it becomes a fund for the curious
or something to be recalled for the historians of science.
The Copernican theory superseded by a better explanation
of the workings of the heavens is no longer of use and
becomes a historical fact. But a work of the imagination,
be it one, two, or three centuries, or even ten removed in
time does not suffer the same fate: it may survive, it may
impose itself, and though created in a past for men long
since dead, it may yet exert a certain power on the present
and so escape time as a work of the exact sciences does
not. Science thus destroys its own past, whereas the work
of the imagination, at least until the idea of progress was
universalized, did not.

It may be that the idea of *perfectionnement* was
modeled upon the progress discernible in the sciences,
but we must not forget that the language then used was
universal in the sense that the vocabulary used to discuss
the exact sciences sometimes was used to discuss the arts,
too. The word *perfectionnement* applies both to the arts
and sciences; it was the ambiguity resulting from this
common usage that Fontenelle cleared up.

Although works of art may be perfect, it does not follow that the more perfect ones must eliminate the lesser
ones, because in the world of science the better solution
negates the others. The idea of perfection, however, did

tend to make taste more and more difficult and demanding. However, the personal element can save the less perfect works from death, though the more perfect works, in the mind of the eighteenth century man of taste, would tend to assume a preponderant place and perhaps even make him look upon his own times as decadent. But the lesser works could still be of historical interest.

At the same time the idea of *perfectionnement* did provide a framework for history of art no longer written in terms of the lives of artists, but on the basis of stylistic values. *Perfectionnement* could thus provide a conventional (in a sense artistic) criterion for the judging of works of art, while the *je ne sais quoi* of pleasure and of artistic genius discernible in the work could counter a too rigid scheme of judging.

It is obvious that the more one ponders such terms as *perfectionnement,* taste, progress, and the relation between the fine arts and the exact sciences, the more one becomes aware that causal connections of a logical order must appear as fantasies imposed by us in the twentieth century upon the hapless eighteenth century amateur no longer able to deny our constructions. The man of taste was not what one might call a rigorous thinker or critic. But why should one have thought about the arts with the philosophical precision we require of the sciences? The eighteenth century had recourse to scholastic distinctions in order to avoid the logical implications of certain evidences. Saint-Evremond may have speculated upon the logical implications of the new universe upon poetry, but the development of taste did not follow his logic. The fine arts remained a realm of personal pleasure; painters continued to people the skies with pagan deities and cupids, most poets went on writing verses not adapted to the Newtonian cosmos, while the notion of taste alone became, for some few minds, an object of philosophical inquiry.

But this inquiry was itself conditioned by the objects of taste; it might readily be argued that the whole Régence generation lived in a world of illusions created by art and taste. We may perhaps go further and say that taste was the answer given to resolve the questions raised by the Quarrel of the Ancients and the Moderns, the problems posed by the implications of the new sciences, and the period's general insistence on reason. Taste became, for a short while, the way whereby men might remain the masters of the new world perceived and created by reason.

PART II
The Structure of Taste

IV

Of Taste Considered as an Aspect of Form and Fashion

Taste in the eighteenth century may, from our perspective, be considered in terms of a structure. Insofar as it concerned a connoisseur, a gentleman, an artist, or even the taste of a philosopher such as Hume or Voltaire, it might be called "subjective" and "relative." But these terms used to describe an eighteenth century gentleman's taste and views on taste can only be termed anachronistic. For a connoisseur knew very well that his taste was not a matter of simple likes and dislikes, though this might be true concerning the palate, or preferences for colors. He knew that taste was formed by art and society and that it was founded upon what he supposed were universal principles. On the whole, taste was bounded in its meaning by referents in the realm of art, society, and history.

Thus, considerations on taste cannot be separated from the world of amateurs and the life of the leisure class of the *Régence* and the reign of Louis XV. Imagination, art, and the pleasures of society provided the delectations desired by that class. Nor can one separate taste from the eighteenth century's general search for happiness. This had begun in the late seventeenth century, perhaps with the weakening of Christianity, the rehabilitation of Epicurus, as it may be discerned in the writings of Saint-Evremond, Fontenelle, and the poetry of Madame Deshoulières and the abbé de Chaulieu. Happiness became a theme of the eighteenth century, changing form and changing, too, its hiding place: during the Revolution Saint-Just and Robespierre meant to make happiness obligatory, while Talleyrand came to regret the happiness of the Old Régime.

The men and women of the *Régence* generation were less difficult than the later revolutionaries and romantics who sought an absolute happiness. In the early eighteenth century happiness was still discussed as an aspect of wisdom, and the happiness one dreamed of was one built on the possible. Not too much was expected of men, but company and conversation were still enjoyable. In the words of Fontenelle the secret of happiness consisted in being at peace with oneself. For Madame du Châtelet, at one time Voltaire's mistress, it was the possession of a mind free from prejudices (though still capable of illusions and passions) and the procuring for oneself of agreeable sensations and sentiments. La Mettrie's famous *Homme machine* was an apology for untrammeled happiness. This search for happiness was at first hardly founded on the great expectations of progress and reason. Rather we are to seek its cause in the eighteenth century's fear of boredom. "L'âme a ses besoins comme le corps," wrote Du Bos, "et l'un des plus grands besoins de l'homme, est celui d'avoir l'esprit occupé." In the eighteenth century the people who mattered, and held power, for whom writers and artists worked, were a leisure class largely without responsibility, and the problem of ennui was a pressing one. The eighteenth century meant to avoid the tragedies and pains caused by the grand passions and ambitions of the former century; but in this avoidance lay the danger of ennui. The problem was resolved through art. As the abbé Du Bos explained in the third chapter of his *Réflexions critiques:*

> Quand les passions réelles et véritables qui procurent à l'âme ses sensations les plus vives, ont des retours si fâcheux, parce que les moments heureux dont elles font jouir, sont suivis de journées si tristes, l'art ne pourrait-il pas trouver le moyen de séparer les mauvaises suites de la plupart des passions d'avec ce qu'elles ont d'agréable? L'art ne pourrait-il pas créer, pour ainsi dire, des êtres d'une nouvelle nature? ne pourrait-il pas produire des objets qui excitassent en nous des passions artificielles, et capables de nous occuper dans le moment que nous les sentons, et incapables de nous causer dans la suite des peines réeles et des afflictions véritables?

Art could enable a man to assume a certain aesthetic distance between himself and life. Art, which to that time had been in the service of religion, royal magnificence, and power, could now be used to make at least some men more at home in the world. It was to become the *décor* of life lived with form. For this new search for happiness, the men of the *Régence* sought a style less imposing, more light, more amusing, than the *Grand Beau*.

The stage of courtly drama, of love and ambition, which in the seventeenth century had still made tragedy possible, was abandoned for the more intimate and less painful comedy of manners. The paintings of the eighteenth century were, thanks to François Lemoyne and his followers, suddenly brighter. Boucher, Natoire, Detroy made the gods more human; the entire world of Olympus, in the *Grand Siècle* still an imposing world, was now turned into light opera. In portraiture the change is fully apparent. The men and women of eighteenth century portraits have an ease and naturalness which sets them off from their more heroic forebears of the *Grand Siècle*. It is as if the decorum of the seventeenth century had become a second nature. The truth is they had changed roles and the style of being a man was no longer associated with exterior form and *décor*. The great wigs were given up for those thought to be closer to nature, and wigs would by the end of the century be given up altogether for natural hair. Chairs for sitting and posing were given more grace, while the sitters themselves took care ever to appear graceful, civilized, *spirituel*. Both men and women liked to have themselves portrayed in their study, writing, reading, engaged with music or some other form of refined and intelligent occupation.

In architecture the same trend may be observed. The palace gave way to the more intimate *hôtel particulier* or town house, and within these the development of the apartment is of special significance. The change in manners, greater civility and social modesty, are reflected in the new architecture. One no longer received guests in the bedroom while one was still in bed, a common practice in the *Grand Siècle* when the bedroom was one of the most important of the house. In its social function the bedroom was replaced by the salon, the bedroom proper by the boudoir, while new rooms were devised for the new life: the private study and, later on in the century, the permanent dining room. The decoration of these apartments evoked a world of grace, charm, finesse, playfulness, and pleasure. It was a time when even names could be revealing of the dream-world constructed with art. Princes and kings called their châteaux *Mon Repos* (Ludwigsburg in Württemberg), *Mon Bijou* and *Sans Souci* (Potsdam), *la Gloriette* (Vienna), *le Petit Trianon* and *Bagatelle*. In Versailles Louis XV found the *grands salons* and immense ceremonial rooms left him by his grandfather unbearable; he built completely new quarters, the *petits appartements,* where he might cease to play the role of king and be himself.

These new rooms of the *appartement* are indicative too of the type of happiness and life one prized in the eighteenth century: the salon for the pleasure of mind, conversation, society, and hospitality; the study for the privacy of one's thought; the dining room for the pleasure of the palate. In all these rooms taste had its form and its function, for a dinner, a conversation, or a work of prose or verse were in fact governed by aesthetic considerations. The boudoir too plays its role in a consideration of this period: woman was the object of a form of love which Stendhal quite aptly called *l'amour-goût,* pleasure without romantic involvements, an exchange of two fantasies and the meeting of two epidermises, as Chamfort put it.

It is not our task to set with precision the time at which this style ceased to be taken to heart. It survived to the French Revolution though a change of taste (and with this, a change of thought and style) forced it to coexist with the new taste for the antique. When the spirit of the *philosophes* and especially of the Encyclopedists triumphed, the rococo style would be associated with a class no longer highly respected. Art would still be subordinated to human ends, but no longer to making men happy in quite the same way: they were to be reformed. Art was to move men to social action, and the search for happiness was to take the form of a search for morality and virtue. Eventually the dream turned into a nightmare. Men still played roles, but the latter had changed; and men were no longer skeptics with a sense of and taste for play, but believers with a taste for heroism. Indeed, by the end of the century the very notion of taste had changed along with the arts.

Taste in the time of the *Régence* and Louis XV was inseparable from worldly skepticism, civility, the flowering of a polite society. A reading of the texts treating of the arts, and the many essays on taste which appeared during this period, shows that for the contemporaries of Voltaire taste was what made life tolerable. It determined the *décor* within which one lived; it allowed one to live with oneself as well as with others; it was the manner of judging the arts as well as the sciences. It was much more than personal preferences for works of art, and it was much more complex than the "aesthetic judgment" philosophers attempted to define in the abstract. Taste was an over-all principle whereby one attempted the creation of a civilized human order. It might be described as the form of thought in a society dominated by art. It was short-lived and was eventually to be replaced by other forms of thought associated with the exact sciences and reason. "En un mot, wrote Charles Rollin of taste, la qualité la plus nécessaire, non seulement pour l'art de parler et pour les sciences, mais pour toute la conduite de la vie, est ce goût, cette prudence, ce discernement, qui apprend en chaque matière et en chaque occasion, ce qu'il faut faire, et comment il faut le faire."[20] Thus understood taste is inseparable from man thinking and acting, thinking and using his judgment. It was not *la raison raisonnante,* it was not the *esprit de géométrie,* but rather Pascal's *esprit de finesse.*

In a more restricted sense, of course, taste was also the soul occupied with beauty and as such it governed the world of the fine arts, including the work of the poet, painter, and amateur. In England it could even determine one's perception or view of external nature, for until Diderot and Rousseau the French did not concern themselves with nature as much as had the English. But taste could also govern what society called *le bon ton* and as such it was the key to *la bonne societé,* and historically defines an entire society whose bases were "aesthetic," formal, and traditional, rather than merely economic. In this respect taste is bound to time and is but an aspect of fashion doomed to pass with the society it defines. Considered as a form of judgment, however, it is perhaps of all times.

Insofar as we are concerned with the eighteenth century, taste as a social phenomenon might perhaps best be discerned in the art of conversation, set in the interior of a salon of the Rue du Faubourg Saint-Honoré.[21] For taste would then have governed not only the subject of conversation, its *élan,* its turns and wit, but also the presence of those invited, their demeanor, manners, dress, the dinner served, the order of the dishes, the wines served, the very *décor* in which the entire assembly met. The gentleman and the lady of quality found their repose, perhaps even their fulfillment in life, in love of society and life lived as art. The anonymous writer of the epitaph to Madame de Verrue, an amateur of the *Régence,* said it all rather well in four lines:

> Ci-gît dans une paix profonde
> Cette dame de volupté
> Qui, pour plus de sûreté
> Fit son paradis dans ce monde.[22]

Considered as the discernment of beauty, as an aspect of aesthetics, taste was tied to the artistic milieu of the period. This was one of amateurs, *curieux,* and artists, of a growing antiquomania and a remarkable and increasing interest in the arts. The seventeenth century had had its collectors and connoisseurs, but the eighteenth century attempted perhaps for the first time to understand in some rational way the "principles" or the reasons of connoisseurship. In this respect the eighteenth century was also the inheritor of developments which had begun in the late seventeenth. The attempt to understand the psychology of connoisseurship is a later aspect of the general attempt to understand the rules of all the arts. It is from this desire to understand that criticism developed in both arts and letters, and as concerns painting, no man did more to help satisfy this desire for understanding than the late seventeenth century amateur and painter Roger de Piles (1635-1709).

Yet the section devoted to this particular problem in his *Idée du peintre parfait* is rather short. The reason is not far to seek: painting, with which he was concerned, is not so much a matter of knowledge as it is of perception. There were, wrote de Piles, only three things to know: what is good and what is bad in a painting? who is the author? is it an original or a copy?

De Piles was especially concerned with the first question and it is in treating this that we find him most interesting in respect to the development of the psychology of artistic judgment. De Piles assumed, much like the classics in the case of creativity, that in order to be able to answer the first question, an amateur had to possess *pénétration et finesse d'esprit*. In short, he had to be intelligent, or to have perception. In addition, however, he also had to know something about the art of painting itself. One is born with or without finesse of mind, but the understanding of the principles governing painting can be acquired. Most of de Piles' writings, in fact, disseminated the type of knowledge that could be acquired about painting, so that those who had perception could exercise their judgment with reason, which meant, in effect, within the limits set by the art being judged. This separation of knowledge from perception corresponds to one also found in the discussion of the requirements for the practice of art, namely skill and genius. *Finesse d'esprit* is thus the complementary of genius: genius creates, invents, imagines; the mechanical ability or skill of the painter executes; the taste of the amateur judges and discerns what is and what is not good in the finished work. Thus most of the questions posed by philosophers in the course of the century and discussed under the heading of taste, genius, or rules, were first posed and resolved, insofar as painting is concerned, by de Piles. He was able to do this because he never treated these matters in the abstract, but always in conjunction with the art of painting, just as in the seventeenth century Boileau and others had resolved those same problems with regard to poetry or prose.

These faculties, to use eighteenth century language, have their specific object in the painting to be evaluated or "tasted." *Finesse d'esprit* and penetration can alone judge of or apprehend the painter's capacity of invention; thus, in painting as in letters, mind speaks to mind. The amateur's knowledge of the art will help judge of the more technical aspects of painting: correctness or elegance of design, disposition, use of colors, chiaroscuro. De Piles drew too fine a line between the mental and mechanical in painting. As the century progressed, the distinction was less sharply drawn; amateurs developed a taste for drawings and sketches wherein they found the painter's genius in all its freshness. Thus the hand was, so to say, put much more closely to the mind than was done in the time of de Piles, who still belonged to the *Grand Siècle,* when subject matter was more important than in a later time which no longer believed in fable and turned instead to decoration.

As for the second and third questions, the identification

of the painting and its being or not being a copy, these depended much more on knowledge of the art generally than did the first question. De Piles insisted on the necessity of a wide acquaintance with art. Many paintings of the same school and the same master had to be seen. For there was another difficulty to be overcome here—the knowledge of a master's hand. Here, too, perception played its part, for a painter's manner was the work of his mind; as in the case of the first question, mind called to mind for understanding and penetration. Here again, however, it was necessary to know a great many paintings by the same hand before judging of the matter. As for the final question regarding copies, there were but three cases to consider: was it a faithful copy in a servile manner? A light, easy, but not faithful copy? Finally, in the most difficult cases, was it both faithful and as easy and light as the original? The first two problems provided no difficulty: one could see which was the copy, which not. The third case posed a problem of discernment, although de Piles was not unduly troubled by the question of originality. A good copy, difficult to tell from the original, was an indication that the copyist had taste, that he had in short been able to penetrate the mind of the painter he copied.

De Piles is of interest to the history of aesthetic theory in another respect. Reading him, one soon becomes aware of the problem of language in discussions of painting. De Piles was forced to borrow terms from philosophy, and he was at great pains to be precise—perhaps so much so as to create a conflict between discourse and painting. The effect is rather curious. His *Cours de peinture par principes,* for example, is a very logically and rigorously organized book. But one may wonder, at the sight of the many paragraphs and subparagraphs, whether this is appropriate to the discussion of painting. He has analyzed the entire art of painting in its several branches as these existed in the seventeenth century. Each branch is subdivided and each subdivision is treated separately. One thus gains the impression of a rather scholastic approach. The whole book seems mechanical and is an excellent example of what the seventeenth century meant by a well-composed book. In fact, de Piles' work is the result of analytical reason exercised on an art which is perhaps not suited to that treatment.

However, one learns eventually to distinguish between his presentation, forced on him by his time, and the thought of this man, whose *esprit* is not dogmatic or doctrinaire. In his works de Piles must use terms which are highly ambiguous (*Vrai* and *Beau* are examples), and he is forced to establish subtle distinctions reminiscent of scholasticism in order to accommodate his taste in painting to terms which are borrowed from another discipline and another order of thought. Thus truth is no longer one truth; he is forced to establish three types in painting: *le vrai simple, le vrai idéal,* and *le vrai parfait.* All these types of truth are in turn thought of as inseparable from comparable types of beauty—simple, ideal, and perfect— and in turn these beauties may be associated with corresponding schools of painting and concepts of nature as realized in painting. The same difficulties of language are met with in his *Dialogue sur le coloris* where, in order to rationally defend his taste for color and Rubens against the supposed preeminence of line and Raphael, de Piles again draws distinctions, this time between *le coloris* and *la couleur,* the former referring to that part of painting concerned with color, the latter to the colors themselves, though these were again subdivided into natural and artificial colors, to wit those of nature and those on the painter's palette. By such distinctions and others between the essential and the accidental of the art, he was able to reach a verbal compromise on the question of the pre-eminence of color or line. But it was, in writing, a purely verbal solution and the question was hardly resolved that way, but rather in the studio and on the whole because the painters of the first half of the eighteenth century paid little attention to artistic doctrines. It was only later in the century that they would pay such attention and consequently alter styles and tastes.

Despite his rather doctrinaire language and approach, de Piles was a man whose judgment, or taste, was not determined by doctrines. He thus belongs as much to the eighteenth as the late seventeenth century and may be counted one of the formative forces of the *Régence* period's taste and thought. He put his view of taste rather well in his *Première conversation sur la connaissance de la peinture*: the man of taste, he wrote, ought to have no prejudices for or against any particular manner of painting; he should listen to the most learned painters and the most skillful connoisseurs, not as oracles, but as men who can very well make mistakes, so that he should adopt their opinions only after having examined them thoroughly and being fully convinced himself. In addition to this, the amateur or connoisseur should see a great many paintings, and not only of the best, but of all types, and where possible with skillful painters—provided these may reason with him and help his mind distinguish between what is and what is not good work.

With de Piles, then, the principles of taste in the arts were already established and the eighteenth century in this realm had only to follow his lead, and to give his type of taste a name, the *goût de comparaison*. De Piles had formulated the psychology of connoisseurship and with this type of judgment the eighteenth century would be able—as long as it mastered emotions—to see its way clear among a multitude of tastes, fancies, fashions, and predilections.

There were a great many amateurs, connoisseurs, and *curieux* in the eighteenth century. They were not all as penetrating as Roger de Piles, though all eventually would use his language and be in some sense inspired by him. The story of these amateurs is known well enough so that it is hardly necessary to repeat it here in great detail. There were two general types, as classified by the amateur Comte de Caylus, namely the connoisseur or amateur himself, who could be admitted to the Academy as an honorary member, and the *curieux*. The amateur corresponded to Roger de Piles' implicit view of him: a man of taste and knowledge of the arts, as well as a protector of them within his means. The *curieux* were less scholarly, much more what their name implied: these were men and ladies who had predilections, tastes for certain schools, certain works, certain subjects to the exclusion of others. Most of these amateurs and *curieux* had collections which were famous and which they opened to those interested in the arts. D'Argenville in his 1755 edition of the *Voyage pittoresque de Paris* cites twenty-nine such collections, apart from works which could be seen in churches, convents, and royal or princely palaces. At the time of the *Régence* the most famous collection was that of Pierre Crozat, who had some 19,000 drawings and some 400 paintings and sculptures, not to mention a splendid library. His home was the meeting place of amateurs, artists, and *curieux;* it was similar to the literary *salon* or *bureau d'esprit.* Other famous amateurs were Mariette, Gersaint (a dealer), Monsieur de Julienne, and La Live de Jully to mention

but the most important. Not all of these amateurs wrote
and it is difficult for us to know how they judged their
paintings. What is known is that they judged rather well
for on the whole they had excellent collections which are
the pride of important museums today. But Mariette
wrote a great deal; his *Abécédario,* a project for a dictionary of painters, allows us to penetrate the mind of an
amateur.

Mariette is quite different from de Piles in part because
he did not write a work of vulgarization, but also because
in reading him it is as if we were allowed into the mind
of a de Piles before the latter had used his notes to com-
pose his book. Mariette's *Abécédario* is more than a dictionary of the lives of painters; it is full of excellent
characterizations of their work. He illustrates rather well
the results of what de Piles called *pénétration et finesse
d'esprit* when this is turned to the appreciation of a
painter's work and mind. The result is a rather unemo-
tional discussion of painters. Mariette asks himself the
question: what can this painter do? He examines his work
with this in mind. His judgment is not based on some a
priori notion of what painting ought to be, nor on some
preference for particular subjects or a particular school.
He judges the painter's skill, invention, color, and brush
work not in a dogmatic way, but within the conventions of
the art of painting. Thus Mariette is an excellent source
for examining the *goût de comparaison* at work. There is
no question, either, in his work of his feelings or his sentiments, in marked contrast to the reactions, for example,
of a Diderot who often gave way to his enthusiasm.
Mariette, in the tradition of de Piles, judges with his
mind, his knowledge of the art, and his sensibility, all
three being joined and sensibility not being confused with
feelings of a personal nature. Mariette too never forgets

that he judges a *tableau,* a work of art subject to certain conventions, whereas the man not specifically a connoisseur of painting, but rather a critic, might be more apt to judge in terms of the subject matter, so that Mariette's opinions are appropriate to the art of painting rather than art in general, or the concept of beauty or the sublime. In this sense he differs somewhat from de Piles insofar as language is concerned, for the latter attempted, as we have seen, to discuss painting in a language more adapted to philosophical subjects. Mariette's language is more suited to his object than that of de Piles. In part this is due to the skepticism of his generation vis-à-vis the general discussion of painting in terms of rationality based upon philosophical concepts. Mariette and his generation were no longer interested in drawing distinctions between the varieties of truth and beauty to be found in the arts. They were interested in discerning between the good and the bad in the works.

Until the late 1740's the world of art was primarily one of amateurs, collectors, and the painters working for them. The members of the Royal Academy of Painting and Sculpture painted without paying too much attention to rules. They repeated at length that the best rule was to follow nature, a device whereby they might be allowed to follow their own bent. But all this was to change in the course of one decade because of the efforts of the amateur Comte de Caylus[23] and the various Directors of Works who instituted Salons on a permanent footing.[24] After 1745 salons were held every two years and these events called forth commentaries upon the state of painting in France. Art criticism was thus born and the amateurs were no longer the sole judges of painting and sculpture. A certain Lafont de Saint-Yenne with his *Réflexions sur quelques causes de l'état présent de la peinture en France,* published in 1746, can properly be called the first art critic. He was but the first of many such critics and his reflections only the first of a ceaseless flow of commentary upon the state of painting which was found to be on the whole unsatisfactory. Reforms effected in the Academy, both in Paris and in its Roman extension, and the development of art criticism and the salons thus went forward side by side. Caylus founded a *Prix d'expression,* encouraged the painting of history, and called for a renewed interest in and veneration of the antique; the Ecole des Elèves protégés was founded in order to give students and candidates for the Academy additional training, and a great many men of letters began to write of painting as if it were a branch of literature. As we shall see, these writings and the call for a greater art were to have a decided influence on painting. For the new writers on art, unlike the amateurs such as de Piles or Mariette, were no longer satisfied to exercise a *goût de comparaison* within the conventions of the art of painting. Rather, they were interested in that much more elusive notion of Good Taste, or *Grand Goût;* with them and the call for a new art, aesthetic speculations finally came into their own.

V

Of Taste, Sentiment, and the Abbé Du Bos

It was banal in the eighteenth century to begin an essay on taste or beauty by declaring that everyone spoke about the one or the other but that few if any could define what the words taste or beauty meant. Let us note in passing, however, that only philosophers felt the need of such definitions. It was also habitual to say in the course of such considerations that both taste and beauty varied in time and place. Yet all this did not prevent numerous essays, dissertations, treatises, discourses, reflections, and occasional thoughts upon these subjects, and later upon the sublime, from being written, published, commented, answered, refuted, or reviewed by Voltaire. Nor did the admitted variability of taste prevent the men and women of the eighteenth century concerned with such matters from supposing that there nevertheless existed a true and false taste, a good and bad taste, just as there was a true and a false beauty.

This seeming contradiction is in part to be explained in that the people who wrote such essays and were concerned with these subjects had learned the scholastic use of distinctions. Although it was the world of Newton and Locke, of empiricism and materialism and the mechanical universe, a world in which—in France at least—men of letters turned away from the teaching of the church and its metaphysics, still it was far from being a pluralistic world. Fable was relegated to the past and the childlike state of mankind's youth, religious faith was explained away, religious institutions looked upon with suspicion, God turned into a clockmaker, but still these rationalists were dualists who believed in a true and a false taste and a true and a false beauty, seeming not to care whether such a dualism did or did not square with taste materially explained. It might be true, scientifically, materially, objectively, that, as Montesquieu put it in his *Essai sur le goût,* "un organe de plus ou de moins dans notre machine nous aurait fait une autre éloquence, une autre poésie" (II, 1241), but what mattered really was the poetry and the eloquence one knew and was called upon to judge. What mattered was not to give in to sensation but precisely to master it. There were those who saw that no judgment of taste, no standard, could be found in its materialistic explanation. Shaftesbury saw the issue quite clearly when he wrote in his *Advice to an Author:* "This indeed is but too certain; that as long as we enjoy a mind; as we have appetites and sense, the fancies of all kinds will be hard at work; and whether we are in company, or alone, they must range full and be active." It was necessary not to let oneself be dominated by one's fancies, passions, or appetites. "For if fancy be left judge of anything, she must be judge of all. Everything is right, if any thing be so, because I fancy it."[25] The whole problem of taste in the eighteenth century consisted in finding an effective answer to the calls which fancy made on men, and the problem was not resolved empirically, but in terms of certain values inseparable from a concept of man and of civilization. Taste in the eighteenth century is explained by the man of taste, and the definition of taste was resolved artistically. It is circular reasoning, but historically this is precisely the case. The man of taste was the man who believed in a certain type of civilization, as incarnated in a certain type of man, and who dared to take pleasure and joy in civilized pleasures. Taste thus implied a certain discipline of leisure. The man of taste was an aristocrat in spirit if not by race, and the judgment of taste was aristocratic rather than democratic, for it was not founded upon the likes or dislikes of a majority. It was precisely this refusal of fancy which prevented the eighteenth century from falling into cultural relativism as the twentieth century did. At the same time it was the insistence upon pleasure which prevented confusion in the realm of the fine arts, so that these were never treated as mere objects, never studied as anything but destined for men in the present and, possibly, as artifacts of old civilizations insofar as they came from a past. Knowledge was the object of the diverse sciences; pleasure and moral instruction without preaching were the aim of the fine arts. "Le goût est dans les Arts, ce que l'Intelligence est dans les Sciences." (Batteux) A standard of taste was thus found; within this very broad standard—for it did include the whole Greco-Roman tradition—was a narrower form of taste directed to specific works of the imagination.

We have seen, as regards this worldly taste, that it could be deprecating to works of other times and places, as it was toward the world of Homer. This was to be circumvented by making the pleasure to be derived from works of the imagination more difficult than those to be gained from the fancy. It was not to be anybody's pleasure, but only of the man willing to learn, demand something of himself, and be generous, yet at the same time still able to keep his judgment and his freedom of choice. This particular critical judgment, or shall we say this "aesthetic" judgment confined to the fine arts, is rather aptly described in a chapter of Lesage's *Gil Blas:* Gil Blas had been to the theater and seen a tragedy by a famous and much applauded playwright (Voltaire). A gentleman from Madrid, who had not applauded, upon being asked his opinion of the piece answered:

> Bien loin de juger d'une pièce que nous entendons pour la première fois, nous nous défions de ses beautés tant qu'elle n'est que dans la bouche des acteurs; quelque bien affectés que nous en soyons, nous suspendons notre jugement jusqu'à ce que nous l'ayons lue; et véritablement, elle ne nous fait pas toujours sur le papier le même plaisir qu'elle nous fait sur la scène.
>
> Nous examinons donc scrupuleusement, poursuivit-il, un poème avant que de l'estimer; la réputation de son auteur, quelque grande qu'elle puisse être, ne peut nous éblouir. Quand Lopé de Vega même et Calderón donnaient des nouveautés, ils trouvaient des juges sévères dans leurs admirateurs qui ne les ont élevés au comble de la gloire qu'après avoir jugé qu'ils en étaient dignes. (Bk. X, ch. v)

We note a suspicion of being swayed by pleasures and taken in by appearances. Criticism' and judgment require an effort, one must suspend one's approval or first impressions; it is this which prevents the man of taste from being the prey of fashion and fancies. We also note there is no question of rules here. The work is esteemed in terms of the effect it has on the connoisseur, and what it is in itself, and not according to a body of rules positing what the work should be like. The rules had become superfluous as soon as taste was accepted as the arbiter of artistic quality and worth, and artistic pleasure became requisite:

Puisque le premier but de la poésie et de la peinture, est de nous toucher, les poèmes et les tableaux ne sont de bons ouvrages, qu'à proportion qu'ils nous émeuvent et qu'ils nous attachent. Un ouvrage qui touche beaucoup, doit être excellent à tout prendre. Par la même raison l'ouvrage qui ne touche point et qui n'attache pas, ne vaut rien, et si la critique n'y trouve pas à reprendre des fautes contre les règles, c'est qu'un ouvrage peut être mauvais sans qu'il y ait des fautes contre les règles, comme un ouvrage plein de fautes contre les règles peut être un ouvrage excellent. (Du Bos, II, 177)

It may seem that one has slipped into impressionistic or subjective criticism. But the suspension of judgment alluded to by Lesage, the act of rereading, or as far as painting is concerned, connoisseurship, can effectively offset a too personal and capricious taste. Further, it might profit us to consider precisely what was meant by *sentiment* insofar as it concerned artistic judgment. For this purpose a short discussion of the views of the abbé Du Bos is essential.

The abbé Jean-Baptiste Du Bos, 1670-1742, diplomat, historian, critic, member of the Académie Française and author of the *Réflexions critiques sur la poésie et sur la peinture,* first published in 1719, deserves more attention than is usually granted him in histories of aesthetics. Diderot was a better writer, in some ways perhaps a more sensitive critic, but he was less original than Du Bos, who had to do what Diderot never had to face, that is, draw the proper conclusions from the recent Battle of the Books and thereby establish criticism. Voltaire knew his worth, corresponded with him and borrowed a great deal from him. We suspect, indeed, that everyone in the eighteenth century who wrote on the arts was more or less put in the position of having to do the same. In the "Appendix" given to the writers of the *Age of Louis XIV,* Voltaire writes:

> Tous les artistes lisent avec fruit ses *Réflexions sur la poésie, la peinture et la musique.* C'est le livre le plus utile qu'on ait jamais écrit sur ces matières chez aucune des nations de l'Europe. Ce qui fait la bonté de cet ouvrage, c'est qu'il n'y a que peu d'erreurs et beaucoup de réflexions vraies, nouvelles, et profondes. Ce n'est pas un livre méthodique; mais l'auteur pense, et fait penser. Il ne savait pourtant pas la musique, il n'avait jamais pu faire de vers, et n'avait pas un tableau; mais il avait beaucoup lu, vu, entendu et réfléchi.

It is admirably put and is a just appraisal. Voltaire was quite right in saying that it is not a methodical book, but then it was a book whose form was in keeping with its subject, a consideration of the arts and society and also the clarification of some of the debates of the times. Du Bos is thus a priceless source for whom would know how his milieu thought about the arts. His *Réflexions critiques* are those of a man of taste, *finesse d'esprit,* and a well-read man, and no such man could have written a systematic treatise. The abbé Batteux, the père André, also wrote on the fine arts and on beauty respectively, but their books were systematic; they were both, however, scholars by profession, whereas Du Bos remained an amateur and perhaps the very form of his reflections explains why French thought on the arts would, in the eighteenth century, differ from English, Scottish, and German treatises on beauty, the sublime, and the aesthetic judgment.

Du Bos never bothered to define beauty and was not interested in constructing a doctrine of taste or of art since the conclusion he had drawn from the recent history of the arts and the quarrels that accompanied them was that it was vain to do so. He could have written, as did Shaftesbury, that "the most ingenious way of becoming foolish is by a system." For the arts belonged to the realm of perception, not the discursive reason; one judged of the value of a work by *sentiment* rather than rules in conformity with the requirements of this reason:

> Le sentiment enseigne bien mieux si l'ouvrage touche, et s'il fait sur nous l'impression qu'il doit faire, que toutes les dissertations composées par les critiques, pour en expliquer le mérite, et pour en calculer les perfections et les défauts. La voie de discussion et d'analyse dont se servent ces Messieurs, est bonne à la vérité, lorsqu'il s'agit de trouver des causes qui font qu'un ouvrage plaît ou ne plaît pas: mais cette voie ne vaut pas celle du sentiment, lorsqu'il s'agit de décider cette question. L'ouvrage plaît-il, ou ne plaît-il pas? L'ouvrage est-il bon ou mauvais en général? C'est la même chose. Le raisonnement ne doit donc intervenir dans le jugement que nous portons sur un poème ou sur un tableau en général, que pour rendre raison de la décision du sentiment, et pour expliquer quelles fautes l'empêchent de plaire, et quels sont les agréments qui le rendent capables d'attacher. (II, 177-78)

To be sure, this type of judgment supposes a man capable of being touched and, furthermore, one who retains his lucidity so that he will be able to know why he is pleased or displeased. The man of taste, or the amateur, is thus no hedonist; he is a critic, though not pedantic; for the pedantic critic judges by way of discussions and theories,

whereas the man of taste does it by way of *finesse d'esprit*.
Du Bos gives us a hint of precisely what he and his
generation meant by *sentiment*. "On a donc raison de dire
communément, qu'avec de l'esprit on se connaît à tout,
car on entend alors par le mot d'esprit, la justesse et la
délicatesse du sentiment." (II, 344-45) We may surmise
that what he calls *sentiment* insofar as it concerns the arts
would perhaps now be called perception.

In his insistence on *sentiment* and his opinion that the
judgment of a work of the imagination, be it painting or
poetry, is the object of perception rather than the discursive reason, Du Bos reacts against the *bête noire* of
seventeenth and eighteenth century French society: the
pédant (become so familiar to those who are acquainted
with the work of Molière), the *scavans en ius,* who always
judged in terms of rules and abstract reasoning. Du Bos
concluded that experts ought not to be the judges of the
fine arts: "Les professeurs qui toute leur vie ont enseigné
la logique, sont-ils ceux qui connaissent le mieux quand un
homme parle de bon sens, et quand il raisonne avec justesse?"

He was the spokesman of an aristocracy of taste, a cultivated élite contemptuous of pedants, not too interested
in scholarship, though some could be erudite scholars who
did not show off their knowledge. It was a milieu rather
skeptical vis-à-vis philosophical systems, philosophical-
metaphysical standards of taste, and Epicurean in orientation. It was this cultivated élite which judged of the fine
arts, rather than the savants as in the days of Louis XIII
and the early years of the reign of his successor. This
public was very restricted. It was confined to those persons
who had "acquis des lumières, soit par la lecture, soit par
le commerce du monde." But the public varied in time and
place, as well as individually. And so taste could hardly

be constant; here one does indeed find relativism, but it is based on cultural and human considerations, not philosophical materialism. Not everyone could be a good judge of a given work or even within certain areas.

Painters and poets themselves could be of little help, for the *gens du métier* were all too often narrow in their views and subject to jealousy and lack of *sentiment*. Only artists of genius were competent judges, but these were rare. There was thus no other way but to fall back on personal judgment, on *sentiment*, and also on history. Caprice was avoided by positing a universal human nature; it was assumed that differences of opinion were the results of difference of language, words ill-used, and differences of convention and historical development, but what all men had in common was perception, or *sentiment*. It followed they must be touched by the same objects in all times and places. The judgment of taste then was, after all, universal provided one penetrated appearances and forgot the discourses of reason. It was accepted, however, that one had to learn to use personal sentiment. Furthermore, the works which had survived time were considered to be useful standards of value: people might be dazzled by novelty for a time, but history would eventually separate the good from the bad and *sentiment* would once more be true and just. For taste was not separated from civility and, as we shall see, it was not for nothing that most men who wrote on taste in the eighteenth century were also historians.

VI

Of Taste, Time, and History

We have already seen that the element of time plays an important role in the judgment of taste. Taste is always exercised in a present conditioned by an artistic past. It is this which helps to explain in part why the men of the eighteenth century wrote the type of history they did. The historical concept of the eighteenth century was the result of a reading of the past in terms of artistic development. The history of the fine arts seemed to be the result of a movement of taste from beauties proper to nature to those proper to the arts, from the touching (and rough) to the perfect. Voltaire wrote:

> Si toute une nation s'est réunie, dans les premiers temps de la culture des beaux arts, à aimer des auteurs pleins de défauts, et méprisés avec le temps, c'est que ces auteurs avaient des beautés naturelles que tout le monde sentaient, et qu'on n'était pas encore à portée de démêler leurs imperfections. Ainsi Lucilius fut chéri des Romains avant qu'Horace l'eût fait oublier; Régnier fut goûté des Français avant que Boileau parût. (Article on "Goût" in "Dictionnaire Philosophique," *Oeuvres,* XIX)

True taste could only be formed by time and a broad acquaintance with the arts, both past and present; it was built upon comparison, not only within the present, but

72

present and past, and it must be understood that there was no artificial break established between past and present until Rousseau rejected the civilization he knew in the name of nature, or until Winckelmann questioned the *goût moderne* in the name of a style he supposed more natural and true than that of his contemporaries. Consequently it can be argued that history informed taste, just as taste made history.

But in marked contrast to this attitude on taste is that of the abbé Batteux, whose treatment of the subject is philosophical and abstract. Voltaire the historian and writer always brings forth critical and historical examples to make his points; Batteux reasons in the abstract and produces purely verbal definitions. The former is a critic, the latter an aesthetician. Batteux contrasted taste to intelligence: "L'intelligence considère ce que les objets sont en eux-mêmes, selon leur essence, sans aucun rapport avec nous. Le goût au contraire ne s'occupe de ces mêmes objets que par rapport à nous." Granted this, we can readily see how aesthetics can be made an abstract science: Batteux does not tell us what objects are involved; he merely poses objects and minds, either considering them with the use of the intelligence or else judging them with the help of taste. Thus a supposedly objective criticism is made possible; for we can readily pose an object of art which we might understand with our intelligence and yet dislike personally. This, however, is not at all what Batteux or anyone else meant in the eighteenth century, for everyone was convinced that art had a moral purpose and the term objective criticism would have been inconceivable at the time.

Intelligence distinguished the true from the false, taste discerned the good from the bad, the excellent from the mediocre, in its objects of choice. Taste as used by Batteux

is something rather specialized; he has distinguished it
from intelligence and tied it to sense impressions: he *feels*
the good and the bad, the excellent and the mediocre, but
he *knows* the true from the false. Neither Du Bos, Voltaire, nor Rollin separated taste from intelligence in this
way. Batteux depends like Du Bos upon feelings, but the
act of "tasting" is now divided into two distinct parts:
first you *feel* the work, and then you judge it. The first
moment is purely physiological, either attraction or repul-
sion; the second moment is more conscious: "Le Goût
doit être un sentiment qui nous avertit si la belle Nature
est bien ou mal imitée." (p. 59) This is quite different
from the type of taste exercised by a Roger de Piles or a
Mariette to judge of paintings. These men did not use
their feelings in the manner the philosophers supposed.
Mariette's *Abécédario* is the work of a man who exercises
his judgment with precision, knowledge of art, and, in a
certain sense, quite coldly—that is, without allowing his
personal feelings to intervene. If men like Mariette could
judge in this manner it was because of something the
philosophers did not mention in their works, to wit, that
they had been acquainted with the arts to begin with for
a long time. The very notion of an aesthetic judgment is
therefore an abstraction to begin with; it is because it is
such that it can be divided into moments.

The division of the aesthetic judgment into moments
has some value: it permits us to distinguish certain direc-
tions in aesthetic writings. Batteux knew very well that
he had neglected the first moment. He called this a
metaphysical problem that he refused to probe: "Je laisse
à la Métaphysique profonde à débrouiller tous les ressorts
secrets de notre âme, et à creuser les principes de ses
opérations. Je n'ai pas besoin d'entrer dans ces discussions
spéculatives, où l'on est aussi obscur que sublime."

(p. 58) Precisely in this direction of metaphysics went the British empiricists and the German philosophers. In defense of Batteux and the other philosophers we may say that they were working under the same disadvantage forced upon Roger de Piles: the discussion of art with the use of an abstract language, one no more suited to discuss painting than it was to discuss or analyze the notion of beauty. This language was oriented to analysis and it was modeled upon the requirements of reason— while the metaphors used, objects attracted or repulsed, were founded upon physics. We may thus say that aesthetics grew out of the attempt to discuss the fine arts and certain human feelings with an inappropriate language. If men like Voltaire, Hume, or Dr. Johnson escaped this trap, it was because they did not think in the abstract; they did not separate art from men, or taste from history and civilization.

We do not think of Voltaire as a special type of historian. He is sometimes referred to as the father of modern history, because he severed fable from fact, but perhaps this is to read him from the perspective of the twentieth century, and so to forget that even when he wrote history, he was a man of taste. This is clear from a little attention to the Preface of *Le Siècle de Louis XIV:*

> Tous les temps ont produit des héros et des politiques; tous les peuples ont éprouvés des révolutions: toutes les histoires sont presque égales pour qui ne veut mettre que des faits dans sa mémoire. Mais quiconque pense, et, ce qui est plus rare, quiconque a du goût, ne compte que quatre siècles dans l'histoire du monde.

Taste, then, also selects from the chaos of history those periods which are thought worthy of exploration and laudation. It is taste which selected the four ages mentioned: they are, for Voltaire, the age of Pericles, Augustus, Leo X, and Louis XIV. Du Bos, who invented the notion of the *Grand Siècle,* calls the first that of Alexander. These four ages we might call the beauties of history, the models worthy of emulation for artists as well as kings and princes. They were the epochs of true taste and genius. These are the times that can never return, but for the man of taste, isolated in the midst of a public avid for novelties and passing fashions, the memory of them is a priceless heritage. They are the centuries of perfection.

The idea of history which begat this notion of great centuries is not that of progress. The idea of *perfectionnement,* borrowed from the arts, is transferred onto history and used to make sense of the past. Furthermore, the *Grands Siècles* defy explanation. They are the result of genius. History manifests a dualism we have already alluded to. Voltaire and Gibbon both repeat that history is but the tale of the crimes and misfortunes of men. But this is so only on the temporal level, that domain where passions, ambitions, and follies reign. The *Grands Siècles,* however, stand above this type of tale, above the chaos created by passions to attain form, taste, and beauty. History might be viewed as a series of oscillations between an ever present and strong tendency to the Gothic and those rare moments, the triumph of reason and will, which are those of perfection. Now the standard of taste is provided precisely by these moments. As Lord Kames wrote in his *Elements of Criticism:* "History informs us, that nothing is more variable than taste in the fine arts: judging by numbers, the Gothic taste of architecture must be preferred before that of Greece, and Chinese taste probably before either: it would be endless to recount the various tastes that have prevailed in different ages with respect to gardening, and still prevail in different countries."[26]

But taste, being a principle of choice and judgment, refuses to accept numbers, so true taste has nothing to do with the Gothic, for in taste as in morals: "we appeal not to the common sense of savages, but of men in their more perfect state; and we make the same appeal in forming the rules that ought to govern the fine arts: in neither can we safely rely on a local or transitory taste; but on what is the most universal and the most lasting among polite nations." The emphasis put on the values of civility explains the link established between the arts and society, the arts and history, and also why it was thought that taste was always in a precarious situation.

The eighteenth century, which produced the *Esprit des Lois* and the *Scienza Nuova,* could hardly help but consider the fine arts in a new way. Vasari might well be considered the father of art history, and his scheme of historical demarcation, borrowed from Petrarch and Alberti, survived him for a long time. But he, in the sixteenth century, could still explain the origin of the arts in terms of near-fable and borrow uncritically from ancient writers and authorities. The Quarrel of the Ancients and Moderns, the impact of Cartesianism on most intellectual endeavors, and the interest in the relation of climate to human institutions and thought led to a different type of art history. If the broad scheme was kept, if it was still believed that the ancients had invented the most important forms and standards of art, if the Middle Ages were still considered a fall away from the Roman world, thinking about the fine arts and their relation to history gained in nuance and complexity—but also in perplexity. The arts were no longer taken for granted; they were no longer lost and found in time. Nor were they solely the work of individuals. Lives of painters and architects were still written, but both writer and reader knew only too well that they and their works had flourished and decayed within certain social and historical contexts.

More important still, there was an awareness of the existence and possible implications of civilizations better known than before. It was a period of European colonization; travelers and explorers like Sir John Chardin and Bernier, as well as the Jesuit missionaries, could write of Persia, India, and China from firsthand knowledge. In view of all these developments in the realm of thought and history, it was no longer possible to explain the origins of the arts as Vasari had done. Just as society and history could be explained in terms of laws—causes and effects—so too the arts were to be subjected to inquiry of an objective sort in order to find the laws that governed their development in time and space.

If the Quarrel of the Ancients and the Moderns served to draw distinctions between science and the fine arts, reflection on the relation of art to society also served to assure the arts and their enjoyment of autonomy. Montesquieu points to the problem very well when he writes, in one of his notebooks: "On ne peut pas dire que les lettres ne soient qu'un amusement d'une certaine partie des citoyens; il faut les regarder sous une autre face. On a remarqué que leur prospérité est si intimement attachée à celle des empires qu'elle en est infailliblement le signe ou la cause." (*Oeuvres,* Pléiade, I, 1054) Those states where letters (by which he meant not only *belles lettres* but also the sciences) are the most cultivated are also the more powerful states. It is true of Europe, Rome, the Empire of the Califs as well as that of the Turks. More particularly, within a single nation, such as France, one can observe that the fortunes of letters are bound to those of power: "Si nous ne jetons les yeux que sur notre France, nous verrons les lettres naître ou s'ensevelir avec sa gloire, donner une lueur sombre sous Charlemagne, et puis s'éteindre, reparaître sous François Ier et suivre l'éclat de notre monarchie. Et, si nous nous bornons au grand règne de Louis XIV, nous verrons que, le temps de ce règne ou la prospérité fut plus grande, le succès des lettres le fut aussi." (I, 1054)

To this pre-Tainian view of the relation of letters to society, Montesquieu coupled one of an internal development of the arts, the notion of *perfectionnement* within genres. Just as societies may rise and fall as the result of physical causes, rather than fortune or providence, so too genres rise and decline and can be explained in terms of certain limits and the very fact that genres are inseparable from their societies. Thus Montesquieu and his contemporaries felt that genres still extant in their time had reached these limits and that everything had been done:

Il est impossible presque de faire de nouvelles tragédies bonnes, parce que presques toutes les bonnes situations sont prises par les premiers auteurs. C'est une mine épuisée pour nous. Il viendra un peuple qui sera, à notre égard, ce que nous sommes à l'égard des Grecs et des Romains. Une nouvelle langue, de nouvelles moeurs, de nouvelles circonstances, feront un nouveau corps de tragédies. Les auteurs prendront de la nature ce que nous y avons déjà pris, ou dans nos auteurs mêmes, et bientôt ils s'épuiseront comme nous nous sommes épuisés. (I, 1225)

Given these two factors, the link between the arts and society and within the arts themselves, and the notion of limited development, it becomes possible to elaborate a theory of art history of a dualistic nature. Montesquieu did not develop such a theory, but his contemporary, the abbé Du Bos, did so with his examination of the *Grands Siècles*. However, the causal relationship established between power and letters, between society and the fine arts, was not as direct, rigorous, and determinable as Montesquieu's speculations might have led one to suppose. Indeed, what Du Bos did was to point to the essential differences between the life of the fine arts and historical development; just as Fontenelle drew important distinctions between the sciences and the fine arts, so Du Bos complemented his work with speculations on the *Grands Siècles*.

Du Bos began by explaining what he meant by the term *Grand Siècle*. It had nothing to do with a time span of a century, but merely with one of those happy times in which the arts flourished in an extraordinary degree: "On est dans l'habitude de dire et d'entendre dire, le siècle d'Auguste, le siècle d'Alexandre, le siècle de Louis le Grand." Let us note in passing that we are dealing with an *extraordinary* flowering of the arts and sciences. Essentially Du Bos had in mind what the comte de Saint-Simon would later call the organic periods of history—those having a certain cultural unity. From the point of view of taste, the *Grands Siècles* are precisely those with taste and style. But it will also appear that we are dealing with centuries or periods dominated by genius. There were four such periods: the centuries of Alexander, Augustus, Leo X, and Louis XIV. Du Bos' first *Grand Siècle* has received support recently from the noted scholar Charles Picard, who regards the Alexandrine period as a veritable *renaissance*.[27] It is apparent that the names associated with the four periods suffice to indicate that we are dealing with the great epochs of classical art. The *Grands Siècles* are discerned in the chaos of history by the man of taste; they are inseparable from classical art. The *Grands Siècles* are the historical justification of taste in the present.

Attempting to explain this flourishing, Du Bos had recourse to two general types of causes: what he calls *causes morales* [or psychological factors] and physical causes. The latter are better described as the physical milieu in which the arts live—what Taine later would call *la race et le milieu*. It is obvious, upon examination, that the use of the word "cause" is confusing, for it turns out that these causes really cannot explain any effects. But of this more later. What, precisely, are the psychological causes Du Bos mentions? They are those which "opèrent en faveur des arts, sans donner réellement plus d'esprit aux artisans, mais qui sont seulement pour les artisans une occasion de perfectionner leur génie, parce que ces causes leur rendent leur travail plus facile, et parce qu'elles les excite par l'émulation et par les récompenses à l'étude et à l'application." (II, 72) We see that if the physical causes are better describable as a physical milieu, then the psychological causes in question can be termed the social milieu conditioning the arts.

Very little is explained by these "causes." What is important is that Du Bos speaks of causes rather than of fortune or the gifts of the gods. There is little advance towards an "explanation." He is unwilling to accept the relativism implied in the Quarrel of the Ancients and the Moderns; he is attempting to establish a universally valid standard of taste. Yet his approach did allow an easing of the difficulties of cultural variation: certain great eras stood out from other times. The wheel of fortune was disguised to become a cyclical theory of history. Du Bos wrote:

Je conclus donc, en me servant des paroles de Tacite, que le monde est sujet à des changements et à des

vicissitudes dans son cours ordinaire, dont le période ne
nous est pas connu, mais dont la révolution ramème
successivement la politesse et la barbarie, les talents de
l'esprit comme la force du corps, et par conséquent les
progrès des arts et des sciences, leur langueur et leur
dépérissement. (II, 175)

There is no question of progress here, though the word
progress is used in regard to the development of the arts;
but it is only a partial progress, that *perfectionnement*
within given genres themselves bound to history. The
perfect moments of the fine arts become for the man of
taste the standard, and thus cultural relativism is avoided,
since these perfect moments are tied to the classical concept of man. Man and his nature are indeed the only con-
stants in this scheme, and man himself is more or less
perfect as he approaches or departs from the models
antiquity provided. In the last analysis the entire scheme
rested on the will to be like the great men of antiquity,
and order in temporal affairs can only be effected by
choosing civility rather than what went under the collective name of Gothic. History is thus an oscillation between
periods of barbarism and civility, rough and near-perfect
moments. The standard of valuation is provided by the
perfect moments, and the choice may well have seemed
justified, to the man of taste of the 1720's, by history,
both past and contemporary.

After all, had not Petrarch written that all history is
but the praise of Rome? The immortality given Rome was
extended to all the *Grands Siècles,* with interesting consequences for the fine arts. For though these were born
in time, subject to time, yet they managed to escape time
because the moment of contemplation or of enjoyment,
the moment of taste was ever in a *present,* even though the

object enjoyed was produced in a past. Thus the illusion of immortality was created; this, in the late seventeenth century and early eighteenth was extended from the individual, to which the Renaissance had granted it, to great historical epochs. We are thus tempted to say that history became possible only because the arts survived, that it was fascination for the arts which led to an interest in the past to which they belonged. Gibbon and Voltaire both repeated that history was the story of the crimes and misfortunes of mankind, but Voltaire added that to the man of taste only four periods were of interest. A dualism was thus introduced into history between the flux of events dominated by passion and appetites, and the perfect moments which were those in which men dominated their passions. The perfect moments were thus a-historical.

Indeed, upon examination of the psychological and physical causes which supposedly elucidate the *Grands Siècles,* it appears that the relations between art and society and between art and history consequently are more complex than would appear. For though it was true the arts depended on history, stability, prosperity, leisure, still they might flourish in the midst of conflict. Du Bos had written, as regards the development of the arts in Rome, that the Romans had begun to write verses only after the Republic had become so strong that the seat of its wars had been extended to foreign soil. Security was thus a psychological condition for the arts. But Voltaire, in his *Essai sur les moeurs* (1764), was struck by the flourishing of the arts in the midst of the Italian wars of the sixteenth century:

Ce qui frappe encore dans ce siècle illustre [that of Leo X], c'est que malgré les guerres que l'ambition excita, et malgré les querelles de religion qui com-

mencaient à troubler les états, ce même génie qui faisait
fleurir les beaux arts à Rome, à Naples, à Florence, à
Venise, à Ferrare, et qui de là portait sa lumière dans
l'Europe, adoucit d'abord les hommes dans presque
toutes les provinces de l'Europe chrétienne. (IV, 91)

All of this does not mean that Voltaire did not generally
agree with Du Bos that the arts were only possible given
a certain stage of development in civilization. But the
two men could not help noticing the exceptions. The arts
needed encouragement—from a sovereign, but also from
the public. Thus it was extremely important that compen-
sation be given for the cultivation of the muses, but
artisans were of such disposition that the giving of com-
pensation was a delicate matter. It did not suffice to
reward artists; the manner in which it was done was as
important as the rewards: "Non seulement," writes Du
Bos, "il faut que les grands maîtres soient récompensés,
mais il faut qu'ils le soient avec distinction. Sans cette distinction, les dons cessent d'être des récompenses, et ils
deviennent un simple salaire commun aux mauvais et
aux bons artisans." (II, 74)

This supposed that the sovereign had the taste to dis-
cern the masters from the mere workers, or mechanics.
Voltaire praised Louis XIV for his taste: "Le grand bon-
heur de la France fut d'avoir dans Louis XIV un roi qui
était né avec du goût." That in fact the king had no such
taste was beside the point; what mattered was that kings
should feel the obligation to have such taste; what mattered was that Louis XV should protect the arts, that he
should endeavor to live up to the standard of his great-
grandfather. But even a monarch who protected the arts
and prosperity did not suffice. The public had to be interested in the arts in order to fulfill the conditions favor-

able to their flowering. Du Bos, considering the Greeks of what he called the century of Alexander (i.e., 349-323 B.C.), supposed them to be a nation of aesthetes: "Le commun de la nation faisait donc alors sa principale occupation de son plaisir, comme le font ceux de nos citoyens qui naissent avec cent mille livres de rente, et le climat heureux de leur patrie les rendaient très sensibles aux plaisirs de l'esprit." (II, 76) This is quite different from the situation which obtained in northern Europe and in which feudalism developed; for a class living solely for and through war was incompatible with a society which would prefer an interest in the arts. But if a military caste was detrimental to the flowering of the fine arts, so too was the attitude of his contemporaries who regarded the arts as mere objects of luxury. In contrast to his own times, "les ouvrages des grands maîtres n'étaient point regardés, dans les temps dont je parle, comme des meubles ordinaires destinés pour embellir les appartements d'un particulier. On les réputait les joyaux d'un Etat et un trésor public, dont la jouissance était due à tous les citoyens." (II, 77)

To Du Bos his contemporaries seemed above all interested not in the arts, but in making fortunes. "Qu'on juge donc de l'ardeur que les peintres et les poètes avaient alors pour perfectionner leurs talents, par l'ardeur que nous voyons dans nos citoyens pour amasser du bien et pour parvenir aux grands emplois d'un Etat." (II, 77) We have a tendency to forget that the times of Watteau and Marivaux were also those of John Law's system and of the Mississippi bubble. His judgment of his contemporaries was not that of a bitter man regretting the past. Simply, it was not a telling judgment because it missed the mark.

Turning to a consideration of the physical causes, Du Bos asked himself: "Sont-ce les libéralités des souverains et les applaudissements des contemporains qui forment les peintres? Ne sont-ce pas plutôt les grands artisans qui provoquent ces libéralités et qui par les merveilles qu'ils enfantent attirent sur leurs arts une attention que le monde n'y faisait pas quand ces arts étaient encore grossiers?" (II, 80) Indeed, such is the case: not the sovereigns but the artists create the great epochs of art and thereby draw the praise of princes. Du Bos considered the physical causes and admitted an element of chance in the conditions for the arts: "Ne saurait-on croire qu'il est des temps où dans le même pays les hommes naissent avec plus d'esprit que dans les temps ordinaires?" (II, 80)

The Quarrel of the Ancients and the Moderns had posed the same question, badly formulated because it was assumed that all wit and genius existed in the remote past of antiquity. Du Bos attributes extraordinary talent, even genius, to his four great periods. The Quarrel between Ancients and Moderns is effectively resolved by replacing it with potential quarrels: imitation versus originality, the Gothic versus the classic, etc. At the same time the psychological factors were reduced in importance. In truth there are areas where, no matter how favorable the psychological causes for art, the latter could not flourish; there are also times in which the same limits exist: "Si Jules II et Léon X avaient régné en Suède, croit-on que leur *munificence* eut formé dans les climats hyperborés des Raphaëls, des Bembes et des Machiavels?" No, and Augustus served by two Maecenases could not in the time of Constantine have brought forth a Titus Livius or a Cicero. All times and all climes were not equally propitious to the flowering of the arts. Du Bos formulated three general reflections on this matter:

Ma première réflexion, c'est qu'il est des pays et des temps où les arts et les lettres ne fleurissent pas, quoique

les causes morales y travaillent à leur avancement avec
activité.

La seconde réflexion, c'est que les arts et les lettres
ne parviennent pas à leur perfection par un progrès lent
et proportionné avec le temps qu'on a employé à leur
culture, mais bien par un progrès subit. . . .

Enfin les grands peintres furent toujours contemporains des grands poètes, et les uns et les autres
vécurent toujours dans le même temps que les plus
grands hommes leurs contemporains. Il a paru que de
leurs jours, je ne sais quel esprit de perfection, se
répandait sur tout le genre humain dans leur patrie.
(II, 81-82)

The *Grands Siècles* thus turned out to be rather unique
moments of European history, for Europe alone holds a
monopoly of true taste.

In Du Bos' writings there is a strong indication that his
thought about art was conditioned by a growing awareness among Europeans that their turn of mind was different from that of other cultures. If in the Renaissance
the Europeans gained a sense of perspective in time (and
thus learned to distinguish between the Middle Ages,
antiquity, and their own times), now, at the end of the
seventeenth century, this self-consciousness and self-knowl-
edge was gained vis-à-vis other cultures in space. They were
acquainted with the existence of other civilizations but
were incapable of understanding these. It is as if they
fixed their own beliefs and tastes into absolute tenets,
formulated as being universally valid, in order to protect
themselves from their growing acquaintance with other
cultures through travel and travel literature. The dualism
established within Europe on the time level, Gothic and

classic, was extended also in space, as regards other civilizations as well.

The term Gothic is thus highly comprehensive. It can mean, as it did for Montesquieu, the state of the arts in their beginnings: "La manière gothique n'est la manière d'aucun peuple particulier; c'est la manière de la naissance ou de la fin de l'art, et nous voyons dans les monuments qui nous restent que le goût gothique régnait dans l'Empire romain bien longtemps avant les inondations des Goths." (I, 966) Stylistically the Gothic is marked by stiffness, hardness, lack of grace. The Egyptian, Chinese, and Indian arts are considered as Gothic and are associated with religion, which for Montesquieu determined the nature of these Gothic arts. Presumably it was the nature of Greek religion which explained why Greek art developed as it did, for the Greeks had learned statuary from the Egyptians. In Europe itself, Catholicism explained why the arts should have been renewed in the Renaissance; a Protestant victory would undoubtedly have deprived Europeans of many fine works. The Gothic belongs really to the barbarians; civilization is measured in terms of the spread of Greco-Roman art and its renewal. For Du Bos the true arts hardly go beyond the northern limit of Holland, and even Dutch art seemed to him *une peinture morfondue,* that is, put to sleep by the cold. As for England, despite a love of painting and great gains to be made by painters in England, it had not yet been capable of producing either a first or second-rate painter. The same observations were applied to Spain; Velásquez was unknown to Du Bos. The milieu in which the fine arts throve was a very restricted one.

Now it is clear that these opinions are partly to be explained by the hold Greco-Roman civilization still exercised on the minds of the educated European classes, formed in Jesuit or Oratorian colleges, nurtured on the classics and the plastic arts of Italy. However, contemporary events seemed to justify the opinion Europeans had of themselves:

> On remarque que les hommes nés en Europe et sur les côtes voisines de l'Europe ont toujours été plus propres que les autres peuples aux arts, aux sciences, et au gouvernement politique. Partout où les Européens ont porté leurs armes, ils ont assujeti les naturels du pays. Les Européens les ont toujours battu quand ils ont pu être dix contre trent. Souvent les Européens les ont défait, quoi qu'ils ne fussent que dix contre cent." (II, 86)

There is no need to mention Alexander and the Romans; the handful of Spaniards and Portuguese sufficed to make the point. True, the Chinese may have discovered gunpowder, but it was the Europeans who perfected its use just as they perfected printing, also discovered by the Chinese. In view of this, why expect the Europeans to consider the arts of other civilizations seriously? It is clear that, considered historically, the discussions bearing on the relativity of taste were academic. Taste was justified by the conviction of cultural superiority: reasoning, philosophical speculation, systematic thought, logic, were merely the adjuncts of a conviction resting on a social phenomenon. True art and its complement, true taste, were a European monopoly, its privileged possession, yet only in certain high moments of history. Art was good insofar as it approached these ideal moments of perfection.

Summing up his considerations of other cultures Du Bos concludes that "on ne saurait s'empêcher d'être de l'opinion de Monsieur de Fontenelle, qui dit, en parlant des lumières et du tour d'esprit des Orientaux: 'En vérité

je crois toujours de plus en plus qu'il y a un certain génie
qui n'a pas encore été hors de notre Europe, ou du moins
qui ne s'en est pas beaucoup éloigné.' " (II, 89-90) Du
Bos has, to clinch his argument, mixed his genres: he
backed an argument concerned with values in the arts by
having recourse to an argument drawn from the physical
sciences. It is partly explainable in that the distinction
between the various arts was not finely drawn. Also,
certain values, such as order, clarity, well conducted
reasoning, were common to both works of the imagination and of science. The separation of the exact sciences
and the arts had not been fully accomplished; both the arts
and the sciences were still served by a common language.

European superiority of art and taste being seemingly
established to the satisfaction of the gentleman of 1720,
one might suppose that would end the matter. But not
so: there was nothing to pride oneself on. It was mere
chance that Europeans possessed this privilege. As for the
Grands Siècles, only artists and poets were worthy of
praise for their flowering, for psychological causes did not
produce genius. And so, contradicting almost all he said,
Du Bos continued to meditate and showed readily enough,
though without explicitly stating as much, that the arts
have their own life and that genius escapes history. The
great men were their own creation (*se sont formés de
leurs propres mains*) and they could not transfer what
they possessed to others. It was true Louis XIV created
academies for the arts of design, but the three French
painters who first brought honor to France—Le Sueur,
Poussin, Le Brun—were formed before the foundation
of these academies and since their establishment "cin-
quante années de soin et de dépenses ont à peine produit
deux ou trois peintres dont les ouvrages soient marqués

au coin de l'immortalité." (II, 94) The times of Louis XIV simply did not have the genius to produce the great painters of the time of Leo X: "Les causes physiques déniaient leur concours aux causes morales." All the cares of Louis XIV merely succeeded in creating "une grande quantité de sculpteurs excellents." The same observations may be applied to letters: they too develop independently of the psychological causes supposedly favoring them. And genius at work produces sudden flowerings, rather than a long and steady development. True, certain masters became illustrious in Italy after the birth of Cimabue, but in 1480 painting still was a rough art in Italy. Perfection only came after that date, with giant strides. Dürer, Holbein, Lucas van Leyden also painted suddenly better than had ever been done before in the North. In poetry and the dramatic arts there was more progress in France between 1635 and 1665 than in the three preceding centuries. The birth, flowering, and decline of a period of art was a short and sudden phenomenon: "L'école de Venise et celle de Florence dégénérèrent en s'anéantirent en soixante ans." (II, 103) All this was independent of psychological causes. Consider the Italy of the seventeenth century: it was more stable, quiet, and peaceful than in the previous century. Yet it produced little of value; its arts were decadent. Rubens appeared at a time when Antwerp had already lost half its commerce and splendor to the new Dutch Republic. As for Rome, its arts were in decay before the barbarians invaded it, as witness the bust of Caracalla, the triumphal arches of the Severi, and the coins of the late Empire. Art thrived in conditions seeming to promise its death. The school of Antwerp flourished in the midst of war; only wars between civilizations could be a serious threat to the life of the fine arts.

Du Bos seemed, in the manner of his day, and before Montesquieu's *Esprit des Lois,* to formulate a sociology of art on a foundation having some semblance of order, rationality, and scientific thought. He had recourse to the notion of causes and formulated reflections in the style of scientific observations. In his manner of posing the problem he was a forerunner of Taine. But, significantly enough, he failed to construct a rigorous system. It may well be that the abbé Du Bos, very well acquainted with the arts readily seen by the man of taste of his day, could not fit even that limited quantity into any sort of pattern of coherence. Thus his reflections on the *Grands Siècles* are further testimony to the growing incapacity to explain the arts by means of preestablished principles, whether a priori or experimental, whether recourse was made to philosophers or scientific formulations. The *Grands Siècles* were the *je ne sais quoi* of history.

PART III

Taste, Art, and Aesthetics

VII

Art Criticism and the Fortunate Ambiguities of Language

The interest in the arts, the innumerable essays on taste and beauty, the writings of men of letters, critics, and scholarly abbés, all had their effect upon taste, fashion, and the arts. Nor was the sense and vision of the past, as discerned in a history conditioned by taste, lost upon the men of the eighteenth century. Both these developments combined to produce a revolution in art and style which amounted to a grandiose if ill-fated attempt to regain a lost grandeur by creating once more a great art founded upon a true and universal taste.

This entire movement toward a new art was in part made possible because the lessons of men like Du Bos and de Piles were not fully accepted or understood, because the generation which effected this change was less skeptical than that of the *Régence*. It was further possible because of a rhetorical concept of the function of art. Taste determined the various limits between the arts, and within these the genres; while the links between artists and public were ruled by the social value of decorum. It is this convention which explains why the abbé Batteux could reduce the fine arts to a single principle, the imitation of *la belle nature*. Critics and philosophers might ask what was meant by *la belle nature,* as did Diderot. Attempts to answer the question by way of definitions in a

95

philosophical, rigorous manner, would lead into difficulties later to be grouped under the general title of aesthetics. But the nonanalytical *curieux* might simply turn to any of the various *Dictionnaires des beaux arts* produced in quantities in the eighteenth century and find the answers. These might not stand rigorous, logical examination, but within the accepted conventions of the times they made sense. There existed an artistic language, with a vocabulary and a usage determined by reference to certain well-known works of art, celebrated masters, and an accepted idea of art history, which provided an objective standard of taste.

It is also the rhetorical nature of art which explains why the first art critics were, seemingly without any doubts as to their competence in the matter, men of letters. It explains why, just as the poets had their *Art of Poetry,* so the painters had to have their *Art of Painting,* also to be written in verse, either in Latin or the vernacular, and either by painters themselves or by men of letters. Since the men of letters knew poetry and fable, it was reasonable to suppose they also knew painting, *ut pictura poesis.* Their role as critics—because they did not suffer from the chimeras of the division of significant form and not very significant content, and because they did not have to seek that elusive aesthetic quality supposedly inherent in the aesthetic object—was facilitated by a vocabulary common to painting as well as to drama, poetry, and even music. Where literary standards, or predominantly literary standards, no longer sufficed, one could always have recourse to the connoisseurs who might use the same language but who had a better eye.

It thus becomes possible to distinguish between art critics, mostly literary men, and connoisseurs, a race or breed apart in the eighteenth century. Both shared the same language, but the latter were better judges of quality than the former. The vocabulary of this common language could be divided into three general categories: words of a rhetorical nature common to all the arts; words of a technical nature proper to painting, yet sometimes also used in the other arts; and finally some abstract words of an ambiguous nature which could mean one thing to the painter and poet, another thing to the public, and still something else to the philosopher. Such words were: taste, genius, beauty, the sublime, imitation. The future science of aesthetics was born of the ambiguities of these terms.

The vocabulary of rhetoric was primarily literary, though some words were borrowed from music. The reason is simple: the aims of the arts were to instruct, delight, and move the spectator *(docere, delectare, movere)*.[28] Music could do two of these perhaps better even than poetry. This insistence on moving the spectator is more important in painting than one would at first suppose. The argument of de Piles and Du Bos to the effect that a good painting is one which moves you is rhetorical and not, as has sometimes been thought by philosophers, borrowed from sensationalist philosophy and a materialist explanation of taste leading to relativity.

By a literary vocabulary we must understand one which has close affinities with social values, forms, and usages. We must not forget that rhetoric still governed society in the French Revolution, that the form and art of this event was rhetorical, that Madame Roland died *à l'antique,* and that the last of the great painters, David, was also the last of the great rhetoricians.[29]

The predominantly rhetorical vocabulary is that which contains such expressions as the nobility of the subject, happiness of invention, reason in the ordering of the parts, correction of style, and such words as style, purity, *gal-imatias,* expression. These terms were used in literature as well as in painting. Allied to this would be a vocabulary derived from the moralists or from psychology and describable perhaps as the vocabulary of the *pathetic fallacy,* a term which could only have been invented in a positivist nineteenth century and a puritan England: thus pictures were gay, sad, or cold, one spoke of the amity, sympathy, antipathy and union or harmony of colors. Terms drawn from music such as accord, concert, harmony, discord, dissonance and discordance were also used, as pointed out by Brunot.[30]

Now the use of this rhetorical vocabulary is limited and as such permits an important differentiation between painting derived from the Roman school and that derived from Venice, Flanders, and Holland; in a sense it is a distinction between academicism and painting of less noble stature; painting which is correct, but leaves one cold, and painting which is "incorrect" but moves the spectator. The rhetorical language is thus less suited to the discussion of the Flemish school and the Dutch than it is to the Italians. The question of the Rules so much discussed in literature has its counterpart in the discussion of painting too: for it is evident that a "correct" painting which can be defined as beautiful, and can be demonstrated academically to be so, may nevertheless leave you unmoved. There came a time in the early eighteenth century when a definable and fixed beauty grew wearisome, as is delightfully brought out in Marivaux's *"Fantaisie de la beauté et du je ne sais quoi."*[31] The latter term, *je ne sais quoi,* marks the flaw in the armor of this rhetorical language, and in the discursive generally, when the latter is used to explain and describe matters pertaining to perception. A competent work of painting or poetry could adequately be explained and described with that language, and yet leave the spectator cold and unconvinced as to its merits.

As for the vocabulary more properly belonging to painting, it derived from Italy and from the studios, and referred either to the entire painting, or parts thereof, and the manner of work of the painter. This was the vocabulary which might appeal to the snobs and so lent itself to satire, as it did for the witty and articulate painter Charles Coypel, who parodied a *curieux* as follows: "Mais, mais, Monsieur, le *caractère*! . . . le caractère, Monsieur, le caractère! Voyez comme les sourcils sont *frappés,* ce front *heurté* et *peint à pleine couleur,* puis *retouché à gras,* pouf, pouf, pouf! Comme ces gens-là faisaient *rouler leur pinceau*! Comme cela est *fouetté*! Ah, Monsieur, cela est *divin*!" (Cited by Brunot, VI, 776; italics mine.)

This jargon, picked up in the ateliers, referred to the manner of working of the painter and drew the sarcasm of Coypel because it is out of place outside the studio, and also because it really tells nothing about either the painting or the art of painting. Rather, such jargon merely tells a great deal about the psychological and social climate of painting.

The vocabulary of the painter was also augmented a great deal from the Italian. Poussin introduced quite a few words into French: *attitude, clair et obscur, grisaille, madone, svelte, virtuoso, représenter au naturel, suavité,* and *barbouiller.*

The use of the epithet was frequent; its use for the description of parts of the art of painting is illustrative of how acutely perceptive *amateurs* and *curieux* could be. To cite but three examples, the *brush,* by which was meant not the instrument alone, but in this case, the hand, could be: easy, light, facile, large, proud, masculine, pale, dry, soft, sure and faithful, lively and witty, sweet, naive and true, full, rich, and fresh. The *color* was said to be true, warm, cool, gentle, hard, hagard, piquant, precious, vigorous, gross, etc. As for the *touch,* the application of the color on the canvas, it could be pure, correct, fine, light, heavy, witty, brilliant, rich, strong, masculine, vigorous, decided, easy, rough, virgin, luminous, etc. Since most of these terms have reference to the sensorial, it is apparent that the impoverishment of the French language in the eighteenth century is a phenomenon perhaps restricted to its use in philosophical and literary critical writings; its more and more abstract nature would eventually make a non-technical perception of painting more difficult, at least for the professional writer or the philosopher. At the same time these terms might indicate why it was often thought that the nonprofessional was a better judge of painting than the artist himself, for the nonprofessional was "closer to nature," meaning that his senses were less dulled.[32] But with this we touch on a problem of greater range, indicated by the use of ambiguous words such as beauty and taste.

The use and the meaning of the terms *beau, goût, sublime* are to be sought less in the dissertations of the philosophers than in the dictionaries of the period. Lacombe's *Dictionnaire portatif des beaux-arts,* Paris, 1755, is most instructive and amusing on this matter.

There is, to begin with, no article on *Beau.* The word is there, but the reader is sent to consult the article on *Choix.* One might suppose that this assures the artist a great deal of latitude, and in a sense it does, but it is nevertheless limited, for *choice* is defined as follows:

C'est, en peinture, la connaissance de ce que la nature a fait de plus beau, et de plus convenable à cet art. Il y a plusieurs peintres qui ont su imiter parfaitement la nature dans les tableaux, mais qui en ont fait un mauvais *choix*. Ce *choix* doit être selon le goût et la manière des Anciens, c'est-à-dire dans le goût de ces magnifiques ouvrages, qui nous ont été conservés, tant des Grecs que des Romains.

We are then told to see the article on *Antique,* which term is fortunately less restrictive than one might suppose, so that the artist once more regains his freedom of choice. But, one might ask, precisely what is taste? The article on *Goût* is more complex than that on *Antique,* but the term is nevertheless clearly defined: It can mean, first of all, merely an artist's inclination or taste for a certain subject, handling, or choice, and as such it can also be called manner (see the article on *Manière*).

Second, there are other meanings, such as *artificial taste,* by which is meant taste formed by the study of other works of art; this taste comes from education, and unless a student learns to fly with his own wings he will always possess merely an artificial taste, as contrasted with another type, *natural taste,* by which is meant not innate taste, but the talent acquired by the sole study of nature, and this taste may be high or low depending upon the subjects chosen; it is a taste particular to Flemish and German painting; there is a further category, the *national taste,* by which is meant beauties and faults proper to the painters of certain nations or schools. (We are told to see the article on *Ecole.*)

Third, there is a second article on *Goût* (*Grand*): "L'on donne ce nom au choix qu'un artiste fait dans ses ouvrages, d'objets grands, extraordinaires, et, en même temps, vraisemblables. Ce *goût* suppose beaucoup d'art, de génie et de jugement, pour instruire, charmer, et surprendre le spectateur, et pour atteindre sûrement au sublime, et au merveilleux."

The conventions upon which the use of language and the psychology of art were built are quite apparent in such a humble work as Lacombe's. There are better dictionaries, to be sure, which amplify the articles here cited. One is Watelet's *Dictionnaire des arts de peinture, sculpture, et gravure,* Paris, 1792. Some of the articles in this work are complete essays in aesthetics and art history. The conventions suppose the Greco-Roman-Italian artistic background and heritage as the standard of taste. Within this, genius has the freedom to create new beauties in the attempt to attain the Grand Style which was supposedly attained by the ancients, but which cannot be defined. The Dutch and Flemish schools did not quite fit in this scheme, but they could be discussed and they could be evaluated, because it was agreed that painting was an imitation of nature, of the visible world. Nature, beauty, taste, the sublime, genius—these ambiguous words were the key to artistic freedom: they had the merit of vagueness, and thus were continually subject to interpretation and were rallying points for the most diverse tendencies in painting.

The existence of this artistic language was no guarantee of good judgment in the evaluation of paintings as such. It was necessary, for art criticism to arise, that men realize that subject matter was not everything. Literary men in judging of poetry and drama were very well aware of this; they judged the use of language as well as the subject matter. Criticism in literature grew from connoisseurship of literary works as such, even though this was not yet highly developed in the eighteenth century. But fine

verses, fine passages of prose, were appreciated for their
artistic worth, not for their moral truth, or message, or
other content. But for a literary man to turn to art criticism it was too easy to stop at an appreciation of the
subject matter alone, without much attention to what was
of particular interest to connoisseurs of painting. It is to
the credit of Diderot that he learned to use the available
artistic language with discretion and a sense of its use
beyond the discussion of the more obvious subject matter
which painting had in common with the other arts. As he
wrote in the letter to Grimm prefacing his *Salon* of 1765:

> J'ai donné le temps à l'impression d'arriver et d'entrer.
> J'ai ouvert mon âme aux effets. Je m'en suis laissé
> pénétrer. . . . J'ai compris ce que c'était que finesse de
> dessin et vérité de nature. J'ai conçu la magie de la
> lumière et des ombres. J'ai connu la couleur. J'ai acquis
> le sentiment de la chair. Seul, j'ai médité ce que j'ai vu
> et entendu; et ces termes de l'art, unité, variété, con-
> traste, symmétrie, ordonnance, composition, caractères,
> expression, si familiers dans ma bouche, si vagues dans
> mon esprit, se sont circonscrits et fixés.[33]

Diderot then acquired a knowledge or an understanding
of the art of painting which was not exterior to it, but
which he learned from the painters themselves. He thus
went beyond the facilities offered by a language common
to all the arts. Once a critic has learned this, has learned
the art of painting *from within,* he will have learned to
master that most difficult precept summed up by Boileau
when he wrote:

> Qui ne sait se borner ne sut jamais écrire.

The ideal art critic is thus a man who knows when to stop

writing. If the *Salons* of Diderot appear lengthy, it is in part because they were addressed to a public which had not seen the paintings. Thus the paintings, before they could be judged and discussed, had to be translated into prose, that is, described in words. There were no photographs. The test of Diderot as art critic came when he had to talk about the type of painting which can hardly be discussed rhetorically, that is, when he had to deal with "pure painting" in a historical period officially dominated by rhetoric—namely, the still life. We know he did rather well when he had to write about Chardin.

Now there is little doubt that one could very well ask: but what does language tell us about a painting? We are once more reminded of Valéry, who (writing about Corot) said that one should always apologize when talking about painting. The language used tells little of the painting, but much about those using the language. Thus the study of the language used in connection with painting will inform us of the audience, the artistic-literary milieu, the artistic psychology of the period, and the society in which this type of language and art grew. A curious reversal appears. The art of painting may be a silent one, but it inevitably calls for comment—acceptance or rejection, love or dislike, judgment and criticism; because, after all, paintings are made by men, and all human actions are subject to counteractions. Painters do not paint for themselves, nor do writers write for themselves. A further point must be noted: a painting not talked about might well be one not worth talking about and the popular idea that it speaks for itself is a *nonsequitur*.

But what does matter is that one speak of painting well, that language be fitting and appropriate to the matter. For this use of language really betrays; to paraphrase Brillat-

Savarin: "Tell me how you speak of painting and I'll tell
you what you are." It will not always tell much about the
painting; it may tell me to look at certain aspects not
noticed before; but as to its deserving acceptance, the reasons, likes, or dislikes, pointing to this or that, cannot
convince; as de Piles and Du Bos saw after the quarrel of
the rules and the discourses of the *Académie,* the personal
acceptance of the painting is a question of *sentiment,* that
is, of perception, not of the *voix de discussion.* Man does
not define or judge the arts; the arts define men.

The relation of painting to language changed in the
course of the eighteenth century.

Poetry and painting both enjoyed a certain innocence
in the seventeenth century and before. Embellishment,
glorification, celebration, ornament, did not have to justify themselves vis-à-vis science and society. Splendor was
accepted as the property of the great as well as of the
church, and the fine arts were not thought of as something
peculiar. The term fine arts is indicative enough of certain
changes in conscience vis-à-vis those arts so classified. It
was, as we have seen in the discussion of the Quarrel of
the Ancients and the Moderns, the awareness of historical change, coupled with a better understanding of the nature of the exact sciences, which drew attention to the
special qualities inherent in the fine arts or works of the
imagination. In a certain sense we may say that until the
advent of the neoclassic style the fine arts were autonomous—not in the sense painting is said to be autonomous
today, but insofar as the arts did not have to serve some
ideal beyond themselves save that other art, the art of
living. We might rephrase all this and simply say that
art was autonomous because for about one generation
man was autonomous: he seemed to exist merely to live

well; he was not in the service of Reason, or Progress, or even God. Later in the eighteenth century, however, this sweetness of life was challenged and the arts were taken up in the challenge and thereby ceased to be autonomous in the sense we have given. The rhetorical nature of the arts was recalled and artists and writers put themselves in the service of society. The arts were to instruct. It is one of the ironies of history that Kant proclaimed the autonomy of art and taste about sixty years too late.

VIII

Reason, Nature, and True Taste: The Neoclassic Style

Throughout the eighteenth century artists talked about nature, taste, and beauty. They asserted continually that art was an imitation of nature, that artists ought to follow nature, that it was ultimately their best guide. Yet while the same words were used throughout the century, there is no escaping the fact that the arts changed so that the meaning of the words was not constant. The *goût moderne* was justified in terms which later served to justify the *retour à l'Antique.* Since the vocabulary was limited and expressive of a closed system of thought, a change in style could only be produced by factors outside the milieu in which the arts were practiced and discussed. Some of the factors which worked for a change of style were undoubtedly the various writings on taste and beauty we have examined in these pages. But the sense of the past and that notion of history tied to the *Grands Siècles* was also a formative factor in the elaboration of the neoclassic style. Then too there was the sense of loss produced by the impact of reason and science on poetry. Thus we may say that by the end of the century, reflection on art and taste and the passing of time had combined to produce a general form of aestheticism.

"J'avoue mon goût pour les Anciens. Cette Antiquité

m'enchante, et je suis porté à dire avec Pline: "C'est à Athènes où vous allez. Respectez leurs Dieux." These thoughts, expressed by Montesquieu in the intimacy of his study and set down in his notebooks, were those of a man who thought, along with many of his generation, that the world had lost the smiling air it once possessed. Such a mood, coupled with the sense of grandeur and nobility associated with the classical past and its later manifestations under Leo X and Louis XIV was instrumental in forming the demand for a more noble and rational style, so that the neoclassic style was in part an attempt to recapture the past, much as Proust would do later in prose, and also attain once more to grandeur by way of the proper imitation of nature.

The relation of the past to the neoclassic style has been stressed by several noted scholars and can hardly be overstressed.[34] It was the sense of the past which made the men of the eighteenth century more aware of archeology and history, altered their style of construction, picturing, designing, gesturing and posing. It was also this increased sense and knowledge of the past which eventually undermined that other craving of the times, the belief in a universally valid taste and beauty. However, it is not to be supposed that this sense of the past amounted to what one would later call historicism or historical relativism. Quite the contrary, the past they looked at gave the men of the eighteenth century a sense of the eternal. Voltaire and Gibbon may have voiced doubts as to rationality in history, but no one concluded that it was absurd. History was not governed by caprice. In the realm of the fine arts, the neoclassic style came to be regarded as embodying a sense of law and reason.

The style can thus be construed as an emanation of the Enlightenment: the style was justified in terms of past artistic models, but also in the name of reason, truth, and nature, these being confused with thoughts of ancient Greece and Rome in the minds of the late eighteenth century antiquarians and men of letters. Though the motifs of the style were drawn from the past, its animating spirit was very much of the Enlightenment. One might, tongue in cheek, even say that its spirit was essentialist, being the manifestation of only one of many eighteenth centuries, in this case one that still believed in universal truths and values, a century less skeptical than the *Régence*.[35]

In the development of this style, which took some three generations to fulfill itself (c. 1750-1830), reason served both as tool and ideal. As the latter it was often confused with nature. The rather abstract notions of the Enlightenment were given an antique garb and the forms of the antique served to limit the meaning of the words reason, nature, beauty, virtue. The result may seem paradoxical to us; for the idea of progress, often associated with the Enlightenment, was progress backwards—to the Greeks who had lived in a world where reason and nature were splendidly and brilliantly united under fortunate and ever serene skies.[36] This paradoxical progress in reverse is, however, easily resolved by the doctrine of imitation: one ought to find inspiration among the ancients in order to equal them. Such an imitation would bring about another great classical period. Progress was construed in terms of the *perfectionnement* of artistic genres.

This construction of a happy past and its artistic resurrection was animated by an enthusiasm akin to religious sentiment. The Enlightenment may have been anti-Christian in its orientation; but it was hardly irreligious in spirit. Voltaire was no atheist. It was largely due to historical circumstances that he saw the *infâme* in the church of his day. Rousseau is an example of a religious man whose feelings for God and nature throve outside humanly created religious institutions. For those who no longer found solace in the church, there remained the moral realm of human action, summed up by the term humanity, and for others there was that vague phenomenon nature. The neoclassic revival, then, is inseparable from a moral revival—a curious compound of sentiment, sentimentalism, cries for virtue, tears, a civic sense, and the desire for heroism.[37]

Before the neoclassic could become a generalized style, the dominant taste had to be discredited. The disgrace of the rococo preceded the elaboration of the new style. The rococo, *rocaille* (or *chicorée,* as Cochin called it) began to be satirized in the late 1740's. This critique of the rococo or *le goût du jour* is found in various discourses and satires. It is dismissed or ridiculed as a mere passing fashion, as unreasonable, tasteless fancy, as imagination run wild. Cochin and Caylus were precursors in this critique; they were echoed by men of letters.[38] The critique of current fashions was paralleled in painting by Caylus' campaign to reinforce academic doctrine, the foundation of the *Ecole des élèves protégés,* his creation of a *Prix d'expression,* and his boosting of history painting. However, it was a far cry from the satire of *chicorée* and *bibelots* to the creation of a new style. In the realm of painting the famous voyage of Soufflot, Cochin and of the Marquis de Marigny to Italy did not immediately sound the return to the antique, nor for that matter did the publication of the discoveries of Herculaneum and Pompeii. Cochin may have ridiculed the rococo style, but for him and others the grand manner in painting still meant the Bolognese school.

Yet a counterstyle was soon to be offered. The *Essai*

sur l'architecture of the abbé Laugier, published in 1753, marks an important date, as does also the very important discovery of the Doric style.[39] Greek architecture was found to be simple, natural, and rational. In the fifties and sixties a flood of books appeared, furnishing architects and decorators with new models. The writings of Winckelmann also were of great weight, for he furnished a renovated doctrine of art where Cochin and others had offered merely satire. Rome plays as important a role here as does the newly discovered Greek Doric and no consideration of the neoclassic could be complete without mention of the architectural books of Piranesi.[40] But Rome is important in another sense: it was once more a school for painters and architects and also for the new type of amateur, the antiquarian. For those interested in the Greek style, Naples and Sicily would be of greater interest; a reform of the French Academy in Rome now made possible trips to Naples for students of painting, architecture, and sculpture. By the 1780's *chicorée* seemed completely wilted. Boucher, Natoire, Fragonard, Van Loo, and their followers were considered painters of a corrupt and false taste.[41] Vien was lauded in France as the reformer of painting, much as Rousseau was to be recognized as one of the new men embodying the new virtue. In Rome Mengs passed as an oracle. Soon David would be recognized as the perfect embodiment of the new spirit. Vien under the Empire would become a Senator. Painters had a new sense of their worth and dignity; they were citizens who played a moral role in society. The painting of history, which had fallen into neglect, was resuscitated; art was finally moral, natural, and reasonable. At the same time the academy had once more become a force in the artistic life of the nation.

The neoclassic was in part the creation of men of

letters, savants and *raisonneurs;* it was perfectly suited
to academic teaching. Vien was praised for his knowledge
of costume and his understanding of history. It was a pity
his laudators had to recognize that his paintings were
somewhat cold. But the neoclassic was suited to something
else, also a product of the Enlightenment—the national
state conceived no longer in terms of a monarchy in which
the king ruled by divine right over his subjects, but in
which a sovereign, either a king or representatives of a
national will, ruled over citizens. Thus the neoclassic was
the prototype of a new form of "official" art.

The neoclassic style was eminently teachable, for it was
justified in terms of a thoroughly rational aesthetic. This
was eloquently expressed by Winckelmann, expounded in
the superb style of Reynold's *Discourses,* and consecrated,
fixed, in the *Dictionnaire des arts de peinture, sculpture et
gravure,* of Watelet, published in 1792. That this style
should have lent itself to an aesthetic is not surprising:
Winckelmann had been a classical scholar before he had
gone to Rome and he continuously quoted Plato. The
beau idéal of Watelet's dictionary, that beauty held up as
the ultimate model for emulation, has certain affinities
with a Platonic concept of beauty. The perfect models of
the Greeks were, in fact, considered as the artistic and
material manifestation of this ideal beauty which in purely
philosophical terms was wholly mental and perfect only
in the mind. Thus the *beau idéal* of the neoclassic period
is another name for de Piles' *beauté parfaite,* or *vrai
parfait.* It is essentially a philosopher's view of beauty,
for the philosopher is, *épris de pureté,* enamored of rationality and in search of universality; he puts the mental
above the grosser sense perceptions. Winckelmann's tour
de force consisted in affixing this rather abstract philosophical type of beauty to the Greek models. These ac-

quired, thereby, universal validity (for reason was universal). A true standard of taste was thus found, fixed, and—paradoxically—change in history and relativity of taste were denied. This was a complete reversal from what had obtained in the early eighteenth century when men were much more aware of historical change, as may be seen in the works of Montesquieu, Voltaire, Du Bos, and also in the works of Roger de Piles, who knew very well that tastes varied in schools and nations.

However, it was only this establishment of an absolute beauty and taste which allowed the men of the later eighteenth century to dismiss the taste of Boucher and Fragonard, just as philosophers had refused to recognize the artistic validity of the Gothic. If true taste was to be found in the imitation of the perfect Greek models, then the styles of the rococo could only be false. And since the true and the false were now known, it followed that the true should be taught in the various academies of art. It is therefore no accident that the development of the neoclassic style is inseparable from a proliferation of academies all over Europe.[42]

The significance of this is most curious. The men responsible had simply forgotten the lessons of the *Grand Siècle*, of men like Boileau, Du Bos, Fontenelle, Voltaire, even Diderot in his better moments—to wit, that art could not be produced by rules; that, in short, the rules were irreversible. It is as if the old distinction between the poetry of painting and the mechanical in painting had been forgotten. It had not, but when it came to teaching art, it was practical to do so. This development of academicism also means that Du Bos' views of the moral causes of the *Grands Siècles* were not taken to heart, for he had argued that the *Grands Siècles* were in a sense products of chance, the results of genius. The moral causes could not foster them; genius could not be produced at will. But to create academies and to strengthen academic teaching is to suppose that art can be, in a certain sense, cultivated in a rational manner, that although genius cannot be produced, it can be favored. This entire academic enterprise and this incursion of the State into art in a rational way meant that art would be created on the basis of rules. The result was an art which answered the requirements of philosophy in the eighteenth century (philosophy here being taken to mean that summed up in the word Enlightenment). Such an art was official art and its typical representative in terms of artistic types was the *grande machine.* This genre of painting was founded upon the highest artistic discipline, the noblest, most learned, and most difficult—history painting; but more, a type of painting which was socially useful, since it was destined to serve as instruction for the new type of man held up for admiration by the philosophers—the moral, virtuous, useful citizen.

It is essential, in order to understand the full novelty of this phenomenon, to compare this type of official art with another called by the same name. The art of Lebrun is also referred to as "official" art. It is quite true too that the art of Lebrun was academic and that the Academy had elaborated a doctrine of art. However, *le Grand Goût,* which is another name for this, was quite different from the art of the late eighteenth century in its intentionality. The art of the period of Lebrun was derived from sources outside of France and it was merely that which most befitted the grandeur of monarchy. This was not exclusive of other tastes, as Roger de Piles knew fully well, as even the other academicians or Louis XIV knew. The grand manner was one which had been formed by great artists; lesser artists tried in vain to derive rules from it to reproduce greatness through academic practice. The aim of such an art was to produce in the spectator a feeling of magnificence; it was destined to glorify and aggrandize the monarch. It was an art of magnificence which had little to do with rationality but featured awe, bravura, and theatricality.

During the rococo period this sense of magnificence was attenuated and turned into pure delight for the eyes, the senses, the amusement of the mind. But in the second half of the eighteenth century, and specifically with the advent of the Comte d'Angiviller as Director of Works, a new art with a novel purpose was fostered. D'Angiviller encouraged the painting of history, but artistic thought under the impact of criticism and philosophy had changed so that the result was quite different.

When Van Der Meulen, Martin des Batailles, or Joseph Parrocel painted battles in the seventeenth century, they did it to celebrate Louis XIV; when Lebrun painted his Alexander series he did it to flatter his king and compare him to the great conqueror of the antique world. When later Boucher, Lemoyne, Natoire, and Detroy were official painters—and as such were also called painters of history—they turned out fable. But by 1770, the period of d'Angiviller, history had changed, and also the very notion of the State. The State had become impersonal, a machine directed by men aware of history and of the importance of the nation. Consequently, the concept of a king as a major subject for painters gave way to that of the citizen, who, like the Romans he "imitated," was destined to play a more active role in the State. History painting came to be regarded as a species of lesson in moral and civic virtue. Historical painting could now draw motifs from the Roman and Greek, but also from the national past. It could serve a purpose in the great philosophical enterprise of the period, the reeducation of mankind. The imitation of Christ was to give way to the imitation of the ancients—more specifically, Roman civic virtue. All this would have been impossible without a change in taste and the new religious enthusiasm of the period.

If the rococo was the delightful style of skeptics and epicureans, of men who believed in genius and doubted of rules, the neoclassic was the style of believers and *antiquomanes,* men who believed in universal rules of taste. It was, in the fine arts, the triumph of the philosophic spirit. This was remarked upon in 1756 by the Italian amateur and writer, Algarotti: "L'esprit philosophique, qui a fait de si grand progrès à notre époque et qui a pénétré dans tous les domaines du savoir, est devenu, en une certaine manière, le censeur des Beaux-Arts et particulièrement de l'architecture."[43] This philosophic spirit had first manifested itself in regard to the arts with the censorship of the rococo; it ended with the edification, or justification, of the neoclassic, which fifty years later was a novel type of official style in France and the style of enlightened despotism in the rest of Europe.

IX

Conclusion: Art, Philosophers, and Aesthetics

There can be little doubt that something of importance happened in the course of the eighteenth century in the realm of thought concerning the fine arts. It has been argued by Cassirer and others that modern aesthetic theory began in the eighteenth century. But the oddity of this phenomenon has not been stressed sufficiently. It is true that Plato and Aristotle had discussed and written on poetry long before the eighteenth century philosophers, British, French, and German. Their ideas had been influential with scholars and philosophers until the seventeenth century, when scholars attempted to legislate to poets and painters. The notion of taste as evolved by Boileau, the Quarrel of the Ancients and the Moderns, the distinctions established between works of the imagination and those of the exact sciences—these amounted in fact to a defeat of philosophical aesthetics (though that word was not used) as derived from Plato and Aristotle. What resulted was not aesthetics but criticism. But philosophers are not easily defeated and a new attempt to found rules of taste, rather than of art, was made in the course of the eighteenth century. Aesthetics as we have come to understand it arose when the philosopher attempted to introduce new philosophical concepts into the realm of taste and the fine arts. The seventeenth century pedant,

117

ridiculed by Molière, kept at a distance in eighteenth century Paris *salons,* once more managed to make his entrance into the world. But he no longer spoke and wrote of rules, but of nature, sentiment, sensation, taste, and aesthetic ideas and genius. He introduced philosophical concepts and problems into an area where these had perhaps no business. In the process, languages were mixed and triplets born: aesthetics, the naturalistic fallacy, and the essentialist fallacy.

In terms of the history of thought in the eighteenth century, aesthetics may be described quite simply as the manner in which philosophers discourse upon beauty, the sublime, taste, and the fine arts. In the British Isles such discourse leads to the naturalistic fallacy; beyond the Rhine it leads to the essentialist fallacy. In either case the fallacy is the result of using habits of thought proper to one type of problem in another area where it is improper. In the British Isles the departure from the mean, or the convention of art, began with a search for the *origins of our ideas of the beautiful and the sublime.* In Germany the departure resulted from a too scrupulous search for pure concepts and the essence of the aesthetic pleasure or the aesthetic judgment.

While German aesthetics has been amply treated in various works on aesthetics, there has been little attempt to go beyond the philosophical language to a core, to what prompted or determined the philosophical language. Were this done, German aesthetic theory of the eighteenth century might seem not as original as has been thought. Kant, for example, is closer in spirit to the seventeenth century than he is to the amateurs and skeptics of the *Régence* period; they had a greater sense of historical variation and change than he did. However, he wrote in the second half of the century, when there were notable changes in attitude toward the rules and toward genius. His concept of genius was restricted to the realm of art, whereas Du Bos, for example, still discussed genius as a quality of mind possible not only in the fine arts, but in all the arts, including the sciences. Thus he spoke of Turenne and Condé as he might have of genius in the fine arts. The differences drawn between art and science in the time of Fontenelle were not as sharp as in the time of Kant.

Kant too, searching for highly refined and accurate definitions, was led to further distinguish between the fine arts and the arts of agreeableness or *arts d'agréments,* which were merely pleasing. Thus he writes that "the universal communicability of a pleasure involves in its very concept that the pleasure is not one of enjoyment arising out of mere sensation, but must be one of reflection. Hence aesthetic art, as art which is beautiful, is one having for its standard the reflective judgment and not organic sensation." (*Critique of Judgment,* Book II, No. 43). Thus the only truly universal—and therefore valid— art is what he calls aesthetic art, precisely that which the artists of the neoclassic period sought in the realm of the *beau idéal.* Art is thereby intellectualized and a very sharp line has been drawn between reflective and organic sensation, one wholly foreign to the men of the rococo period.

Is Kant not in fact creating the straw men we alluded to in our introduction? The classical genres and their hierarchy allowed for much more variety than Kant's distinctions. In stating that the fine arts must be universal in their appeal, he introduces nothing novel. This had been one of the classical tenets of the *Grand Siècle.* But what is novel is his supposition that such universality is of an intellectual variety. Du Bos had thought the opposite: if works of the imagination survived time, it was because they could still touch us.

Then too, are there arts merely addressed to organic sensations? Molière's *Misanthrope* affords a pleasure different from that of the *Fourberies de Scapin,* but must we follow Boileau and fail to recognize Molière in the latter or must we conclude that only the former deserves to be considered true art? Kant is a purist such as no playwright or artist could be. One might even show that Kant substituted for the old academic hierarchy of genres one based on extra-artistic notions. The more intellectual the art, such as poetry, the higher its place in the hierarchy. Music and painting, appealing directly to the senses, would be lower down in the scale. This contemporary of Mozart raises grave doubts about the taste or judgments of aestheticians. He missed the point that both music and painting also require intelligence. Indeed, he went as far as to doubt that they could be regarded as fine arts. In general, then, the closer an art resembled philosophy and pure thought, the higher it was in his estimation.

What he has to say concerning genius and the rules of art is a mere restatement in conceptual language of what had been repeated throughout the eighteenth century. He defines genius as follows:

Thus it may be seen that *genius* (1) is a *talent* for producing that for which no definite rule can be given; and not an aptitude in the way of cleverness for what can be learned according to some rule; and that consequently *originality* must be its primary property. (2) Since there may also be original nonsense, its products must at the same time be models, i.e., *exemplary;* and, consequently, though not themselves derived from imitation, they must serve that purpose for others, i.e., as standards of rule and of estimating. (3) It cannot indicate scientifically how to bring about its product, but rather gives the rules as *nature*.

In all this he merely restates de Piles, Reynolds, and others, men who were practicing artists and poets and who had learned in the seventeenth century that art could not be produced by rules. However, Kant stated all this in a learned manner and thus gave the illusion that he had given the final word on the matter. In fact, he merely changed languages and renamed the *je ne sais quoi*, calling it an aesthetic idea and defining this as "that representation of the imagination which induces much thought, yet without the possibility of any definite thought whatever, i.e., *concept*, being adequate to it, and which language, consequently, can never get quite on a level with or render completely intelligible."

If in the British Isles speculation upon beauty, taste, and the sublime led to a consideration of sensations, if in the Germanies it led to the definition of faculties and categories of the understanding, in both cases aesthetics remained a branch of philosophy, practiced by philosophers, understood by philosophers interested above all in the problem of cognition. In the course of this process and enterprise the vocabulary used in reference to the arts changed: words like imitation, nature, genius, beauty, and the sublime no longer meant the same thing they had to artists or poets.

For it is possible to write a treatise on beauty without referring either to the arts or to nature. A professor of philosophy in the eighteenth century may have thought of beauty in close connection with a pure idea of beauty; a British empiricist might write of it in terms of sensations and feelings of pleasure or displeasure. The Germans intellectualized beauty; the English materialized it; the French drew distinctions. For a painter, beauty was something quite different from all these types of abstract beauties: it referred to certain specific works belonging to a certain school, or it might even be certain parts of a painting, amid others less successfully brought forth. To a poet it might be something else again. When practicing poets or painters spoke of beauty, they had in mind certain models from the ancients or the moderns. The various pocket dictionaries of fine arts put out in the eighteenth century were remarkably clear and provided an adequate language for the discussion of paintings. The differences between the languages, and consequently between the aesthetic as a realm of philosophical discourse and the artistic as the realm of judgment, are clear in Diderot's *Recherches philosophiques sur l'origine et la nature du beau* and his *Salons.* Obviously two different matters are involved here: in the former he writes as a philosopher about philosophical problems; in the latter he writes as a critic. In either case the problems and the language derive from, or are stipulated by, the object of reflection and neither mix. It is when the languages are mixed that confusion arises. If one does keep the distinction in mind it becomes apparent that the history of aesthetics is one thing, and the history of criticism and of tastes are another. When these various histories do mix it is apparent that taste is no longer operative, or we might say, that the aesthetic judgment, that faculty of discerning what is or is not fitting, no longer operates. For as we have seen, the word taste, as used by men like Du Bos or Rollin, regulated much more than one's perception of the beautiful in the arts or in nature. Such a breakdown of taste occurred in the course of the eighteenth century due in part to the impact of empiricism and metaphysical speculation. It was out of this change that aesthetics arose, along with the essentialist fallacy, derived from speculations upon religious matters, and the naturalistic fallacy, derived from speculations concerning the human understanding.

We ought to keep in mind that the Quarrel of the Ancients and Moderns, the breakdown of the supposed authority of the rules, and the separation of the works of imagination from those of the exact sciences, were contemporary with another important movement in the realm of religion, namely the *querelle du pur amour*, or Quietism and Pietism. We ought further not to forget that the men involved in all these questions were the same. Even though they might be separated in time or space, they corresponded or inherited problems posed by the previous generation of Descartes. The term republic of letters should be kept in mind. Also, new editions of works were being issued as if they were still up to date. Thus it is significant that Kames in the 1760's still discussed Le Bossu, a seventeenth century savant, as if one still cared about the rules; that Dr. Johnson in Britain still brought up the question of these same rules in his "Preface to Shakespeare" in a time when one could in France, after the Quarrel, call these a dead issue. Thus we ought not to be surprised that Kant merely summarized, reconciled, or systematized the various writings on criticism, beauty, and the sublime which made up the heritage of about a century and a half of repetitious writing.

In view of this unity of thought, which is that of a unity of problems, one has been struck by the close resemblance between the question of the disinterested love of God, or the *querelle du pur amour,* and that of aesthetic pleasure. Both these problems are resolved by having recourse to definitions. As Leibniz wrote Burnet in 1697, "pour décider de telles questions il faut avoir de bonnes définitions. Vous trouverez ma définition dans la préface de mon code diplomatique, où je dis: *amare est felicitate alterius delectari,* trouver son plaisir dans la félicité d'autrui. Et par cette définition on peut résoudre cette grande question, comment l'amour véritable peut être désintéressé, quoique cependant il soit vrai que nous ne faisons rien que pour notre bien. C'est que toutes les choses que nous désirons par elles-mêmes et sans aucune vue d'intérêt, sont d'une nature à nous donner du plaisir par leur excellentes qualités, de sorte que la félicité de l'objet aimé entre dans la nôtre." The similarity between this problem of a disinterested love of God and the disinterested aesthetic pleasure is striking. Just as in questions of the proofs of God and the reasons for faith, so in questions of aesthetic judgment there are reasons which may be explained and others which may not, while aesthetic contemplation, defined by Kant as "a judgment which is indifferent as to the existence of an object, and only decides how its character stands with the feeling of pleasure and displeasure" has some striking parallels with the pietistic *oraison de simple regard,* in which one abandons oneself totally, avoids all desire, and becomes akin to a dead body waiting to be moved by God rather than by individual will. Thus pietistic contemplation and the aesthetic contemplation have in common passivity. In both cases there is posited a subject and an object; the problem, probably derived from the mind-body question, is that of the relation between the object and the subject: if the judgment of the object is disinterested it is aesthetic; if the contemplation of God is free of all *propriété et activité,* that is, of all the forms set by the cult and all motion coming from the subject, it is pure. Both the pietist and the pure aesthetician, in this particular case Kant, push the relation of subject to object to a point where it supposes man to be an angel, a condition hardly possible for men.

If the direction given discourse on beauty in Germany led to what we might call an aesthetics for angels, in the British Isles the investigation of the sources of beauty and the subime led to an aesthetics for economists. In both cases aesthetics is led away from the arts, though Kant's writings on beauty and the fine arts are a philosophical rendering of the classical position. But in Britain the confusion of art and nature became more apparent, and the aesthetic judgment or pleasure was reduced to a question of sensations. Indeed, an attempt was made by Burke, Kames, and Alison to determine rules of taste experimentally so that British empirical aesthetics of the eighteenth century assumed a character rather similar to the disputes between pedants and poets of the seventeenth century. The difference was that the rules were no longer to be founded on Aristotle and Horace, but on human nature, and since the approach of the British empiricists was analytical, the question of taste was reduced to one of sensations, a position which "ignores, among other things, the difference between life and art, and the whole question of aesthetic 'significance.' "[44]

Burke attempted to find the rules or laws which governed taste, the word here being taken in the physiological sense though not reduced to the taste of the palate alone, but including our physical as well as mental preferences. Burke could not accept what poets, painters, amateurs had readily accepted since the Renaissance, indeed, for a time longer than that, namely variety of taste. Thus he writes that "it is probable that the standard both of reason and Taste is the same in all human creatures. For if it were not some principle of judgment as well as sentiment common to all mankind, no hold could possibly be taken either on their reason or their passions, sufficient to maintain the ordinary correspondence of life. It appears indeed to be generally acknowledged that with regard to truth and falsehood there is something fixed." (*A Philosophical Enquiry,* p.11)

What is discernible here is the abstract, rational man of the eighteenth century *philosophes;* be he British, French, or German, it is the *homme-machine sensible et raisonnable,* universal because abstract; a man no longer various, capricious, sinful, bored, as well as reasonable. Burke posed an abstract man in a universe founded as rational. For he saw the alternative clearly enough: if men were not rational, if the world were not governed by law, then all would be caprice, all would be vain. Burke's concept of taste was in fact founded upon an act of faith in rationality: "For if Taste has no fixed principles, if the imagination is not affected according to some invariable and certain laws, our labour is like to be employed to very little purpose; as it must be judged a useless, if not an absurd undertaking, to lay down rules for caprice, and to set up for a legislator of whims and fancies." (p.12) Burke was not sufficiently skeptical to accept what Hume could accept, and before Hume, Fontenelle, whose attitude to the rules was quite different; he considered them amusing but really useless speculations:

Les spéculations sur la nature des règles ne donnent point de génie à ceux qui en manquent, elles n'aident pas beaucoup ceux qui en ont, et le plus souvent même les gens de génie sont incapables d'être aidés par les spéculations. A quoi donc sont-elles bonnes? A faire remonter jusqu'aux premières idées du beau quelques gens qui aiment le raisonnement, et qui se plaisent à réduire sous l'empire de la philosophie les choses qui en paraissent les plus indépendantes, et que l'on croit communément abandonnées à la bizarrerie des goûts." (*Oeuvres,* Amsterdam, 1754, 375-76)

The rules were irreversible; they were purely speculative, a species of game, verbal constructions of no use to those who in fact fashioned taste by creating works of art.

All this does not mean that Burke's work on taste was unimportant; the contrary is true, for the history of thought is, after all, not always the history of reason, but of error as well. Burke's work was influential. Rather than distinguish between the social and the personal, between what in a work of art belonged to past convention, and what belonged to present pleasure, Burke shifted attention away from criticism to psychological considerations of a rather mechanical nature. This led to what would later be termed aesthetics from below. At the same time, since he wrote about the feelings rather than the reason of our artistic judgments, he did not distinguish between the effects of pleasure produced by the beauties of art and those of nature. British aesthetics, then, is an aesthetics of nature and the naturalistic fallacy.[45] The confusion caused would only be unraveled in the nineteenth century. Baudelaire's reaction against nature, for example, is a case in point—one among many others. The attempt to explain the feelings of beauty and the sublime on a purely material basis blurred the differences between various types of beauties in art and also the various nuances of the word as we find it in Father André's treatise which, if scholastic, at least possesses the merit of clarity and of avoiding the confusions of the empiricists. In view of these confusions, these blurrings of differences, and above all the confusion of art and nature in abstract writings on the feelings, the history of aesthetics in the eighteenth century has often been misread. For example, it has been written that "between the *Essay on Criticism* and Burke's *Enquiry*, the aesthetic experience was broken down into the two categories of the beautiful and the sublime, and while the first remained true to neoclassic taste, the latter became more and more associated with aspects of the external world which could not be approved by orthodox taste, but which the younger generation was determined to enjoy, and with the strongly pathetic, which still enjoyed a theoretical respectability by virtue of its Longinian origin."[46] This is hardly stating the case well. The history of fashions and tastes is more complicated than that; the words beauty and sublime were often used interchangeably. The Romans were sublime to the men who eventually made the French Revolution, while Roman matrons were beautiful. Madame Roland's death was not only heroic, but sublime.

It is quite true that Burke shifted attention to exterior nature with his writings on the sublime and thereby may have, along with Jean-Jacques Rousseau and others, started a fashion for walks in the country and grand gestures before sublime landscapes, thus making a fortune for the Swiss: but a walk in the country, an outing on Lake Geneva, are one thing, whereas a painting of a landscape defined as sublime or a view of Lake Geneva by Liotard or Töpffer are another and because we know the latter two are works by men, the feelings we have about them will be infinitely more complicated than the feelings we may have for natural sites. It is also erroneous to suppose that beauty is neoclassic. There were subjects of horror in the arts which were nevertheless called beautiful because of what we might, despite the dangers inherent in the term, call aesthetic distance. Boileau put it as follows in his *Art poétique:*

> Il n'est point de serpent, ni de monstre odieux,
> Qui, par l'art imité, ne puisse plaire aux yeux;
> D'un pinceau délicat l'artifice agréable
> Du plus affreux objet fait un objet aimable.

The seventeenth century had not confused art and nature; it was much more subtle about feelings than either Burke, Home, or Alison, while the men of the *Régence* knew very well that taste was not exercised by the feelings, but mind.

The men of the *Régence,* the amateurs, the artists, the poets, were men willing to accept the conditions set by art in order to consider taste and judgment, and having done this, they were willing to take risks and back their feelings with reasons of connoisseurship. But the British empiricists sought certainty, they sought to establish rational and scientific grounds for rules and taste.

Home thought that a *rational science of criticism* would not only be scientific and founded on true rules, but further, it would be useful to the individual as well as to society. This was justified in terms of a hierarchy of senses made for human happiness by means of a sweet and easy transition "from corporeal pleasures to the more refined pleasures of sense, and no less so, from these, to the exalted pleasures of morality and religion." This was no novel idea. Addison had already hinted at it in his papers on the *Pleasures of the Imagination.* In the third of these papers he speculates on why men should be pleased by the great, the new, and the beautiful. He admits that we cannot know the causes of these pleasures but assumes that our admiration is tied to God's creation. Things are beautiful or pleasing because God so made them and thereby intended to make the "whole creation more gay and delightful." Ultimately, then, it is possible to tie aesthetic delight to morality and also to God's work.

Home also makes of self-cultivation a moral obligation, though he says that in so doing we are in fact seconding the purposes of nature: "We stand . . . engaged in honor, as well as interest, to second the purposes of nature, by cultivating the pleasures of the eye and ear; those especially that require extraordinary culture—such as arise from poetry, painting, sculpture, music, gardening and architecture." Taste for the fine arts and the moral sense are thus allied and both are "rooted in human nature, and governed by principles common to all men." The cultivation of this taste will procure "to a man, so much mental enjoyment, that, in order to be occupied, he is not tempted to deliver up his youth to hunting, gaming, drinking; nor his middle age to ambition; nor his old age to avarice." At this point, Home's idea of men appears somewhat simple.

One will find much the same attitude in Archibald Alison's *Essays on the Nature and Principles of Taste* (1790). Here it is even argued that an investigation of taste will also be useful to the artist: "Without a just and accurate conception of the nature of these qualities (those which produce the emotions of taste), the *artist* must be unable to determine whether the beauty he creates is temporary or permanent, whether adapted to the accidental prejudices of his age, or to the uniform constitution of the human mind; and whatever the science of *criticism* can afford for the improvement or correction of taste, must altogether depend upon the previous knowledge of the nature and laws of this faculty." Alison does not seem to have asked himself how it was artists had managed for some two thousand years without knowledge of the just and accurate concept of the principles of taste. But then he may have confused art and nature and been incapable of grasping the arts of aristocratic Europe.

In a sense both Home and Alison democratize the arts, first by founding taste upon the senses possessed by all men, rather than artistic judgment; and second by making of art an extension of nature accessible to all. This is well brought out by Alison in his Introduction: "I feel it incumbent on me . . . to inform my readers that I am to employ, in these inquiries, a different kind of evidence from what has usually been employed by writers upon these subjects, and that my illustrations will be derived much less from the compositions of the fine arts than from the appearances of common nature, and the experience of common men. If the fine arts are, in reality, arts of imitation, their principles are to be sought for in the subject they imitate; and it is ever to be remembered [and he is quoting from Addison] 'that music, architecture, and painting, as well as poetry and oratory, are to deduce their laws and rules from the general sense and taste of mankind, and not from the principles of these arts themselves: in other words that taste is not to conform to the art, but the art to the taste.' " It is a remarkable attitude, for it put into question the hard-won freedom of poets and painters to

> Let such teach others who themselves excel,
> And censure freely to have written well.

Contrasted with the British and German positions, French writing on the fine arts remained closely linked to the classical position and did not lead to a separate science of aesthetics, but to a refinement of artistic judgment, and the best summary of eighteenth century French thought on this matter was the abbé Du Bos. The course of eighteenth century French writing on the arts, and perhaps even of French writing on the arts in general was set by him and it is noteworthy that he did not define beauty, nor mix the beauty of nature with that of the arts. French eighteenth century aesthetics remained tied to criticism and connoisseurship and the distinction between the exact sciences and the fine arts, set in the course of the *Querelle des Anciens et des Modernes,* was not forgotten.

Viewed within the general context of the artistic and social milieu of the eighteenth century, aesthetics considered as a branch of philosophy was a marginal activity carried on by a few rather isolated individuals in centers often removed from artistic activity and taste. Where aesthetics influenced art the result was not always fortunate. The neoclassic style is an instance of this: it is a manifestation of aestheticism and academicism. On the whole, however, we may say that the history of aesthetics is one thing, that of art another. Perhaps this is no longer the case today but until the advent of the neoclassic style, what kept art and aesthetics apart was precisely the object of study of the philosophers, namely taste or aesthetic judgment which assigned each discipline and activity its proper area of competence and its limits.

Thinking upon what has been written in the foregoing pages, we may sum up our argument as follows:

In the late seventeenth century and in the early eighteenth, certain thinkers discovered the historical nature of art. Since the arts, by their rhetorical nature, had till then been discussed as but one aspect of social, moral, and religious values they were caught up in the entire movement of ideas called the Enlightenment. The historical nature of the arts conflicted with a traditional approach to their discussion founded upon supposedly universal and valid rules and standards of judgment. A conflict thus arose in the minds of men between the supposition of universal standards of truth and rules of art, and historical evidence to the contrary. The conflict was resolved by taste: a duality of art was posed. The arts were historical in nature, there were no universally valid rules; but taste might nevertheless create order out of historical chaos by being able to distinguish between what in a work of art was specifically historical and what was universal—its potential of pleasing men of various places and times.

This compromise supposed the existence of a leisure class well acquainted with the arts and living a rather epicurean life. Yet the very discovery of the historical nature and importance of art, coupled with the concept of its old rhetorical nature to the effect that art can be used as moral instruction, combined to undermine and eventually replace this epicurean *dix-huitième* and its style. An attempt was made to create a style in conformity with the lessons drawn from art history as realized in the notion of the *Grands Siècles;* the result was the neoclassic style.

The entire discussion of art, taste, beauty, genius, and the sublime may be subsumed under the name of aesthetics, within which one must distinguish between a tendency to treat these questions in metaphysical terms and another to remain on the level of criticism. Insofar as the neoclassic style attempted to realize the *beau idéal,* it was influenced, at least in its intention and justification, by the new considerations on art; insofar as the rococo was a style which did not pretend beyond a human world, it was founded upon artistic rather than aesthetic principles. The rococo proceeded from previous art; the neoclassic proceeded from a very restricted choice of previous art determined and justified by the new aesthetic of universal pretensions.

What remains from this history, besides the works of art loved and discussed at the time, is the remembrance of a high level of civilization, the knowledge of the historical nature of art, and a concept of taste still valid and constantly in use today, namely the *goût de comparaison*. As for aesthetics, it may be considered as a survival from that period, the remains of an attempt to subsume art and taste under universal and rational principles, a science without an object, turned in upon itself; or a science with too many objects subsumed under the word art and begetting thereby a body of highly abstract writings of doubtful utility.

Bibliographical Notes

1. Ernst Cassirer, *The Philosophy of the Enlightenment*, Princeton Univ. Press, 1951, p. 227. See also, for this renewed interest in the origins of aesthetic theory, the articles of Jerome Stolnitz, "On the Significance of Lord Shaftesbury in Modern Aesthetic Theory," *Philosophical Quarterly*, Vol. 11, no. 43, 97-113; "Beauty: Some Stages in the History of an Idea," *Journal of the History of Ideas*, XXII, no. 2, 185-204; and "On the Origins of 'Aesthetic Disinterestedness,' " in *Journal of Aesthetics and Art Criticism*, XX, no. 2, 131-43. Raymond Bayer in his recently published *Histoire de l'Esthétique*, Paris, 1961, gives considerable space to the British eighteenth century empiricists.

I am taking the word aesthetics to mean the study of beauty and the arts as a branch of philosophy. See Ruth Saw and Harold Osborn, "Aesthetics as a Branch of Philosophy," *British Journal of Aesthetics*, I, no. 1, pp. 8 ff.

2. Paris, 1946, II, 118.

3. Armand Nivelle, *Kunst und Dichtungstheorien zwischen Aufklärung und Klassik*, Berlin, 1960, p. 234. This is an excellent study of German aesthetic theories. It can, however, be usefully supplemented by Emil Ermatinger's *Dichtung und Geistesleben der Deutschen Schweiz*, Munich, 1933, for the Swiss theoreticians Bodmer and Breitinger. For the period preceding Baumgarten, see the section on Leibniz in Bayer, *op. cit.* in note 1, 147-51.

4. Diderot, *Oeuvres esthétiques,* ed. Paul Vernière, Paris, n.d., p. 415. Diderot wrote only one formal treatise on aesthetic theory, the article "Beau" for the *Encyclopédie,* from which we

135

have quoted. Contradictions in Diderot's aesthetics, not to mention in his thought generally, have been the subject of several works, notable among which are Yvon Belaval's *L'Esthétique sans paradoxe de Diderot,* Paris, 1950, and L. G. Crocker's *Two Diderot Studies: Ethics and Esthetics,* Baltimore, 1952.

Father Ives Marie André, S.J., published the work alluded to by Diderot in 1741. It was entitled *Essai sur le beau, où l'on examine en quoi consiste précisément le beau dans le physique, dans le moral, dans les ouvrages d'esprit et dans la musique.* This work was edited many times in the eighteenth century and was even re-edited by Victor Cousin in the nineteenth. It is made up of academic discourses, is extremely well organized, clear, systematic, well constructed, well reasoned, and Cartesian in its rigor and organization. It further has the merit of drawing some useful distinctions; as will be seen by the title itself, there are differences to be taken into account, and Father André points to the differences between the Beauty of the theologians, metaphysicians, artists, and critics. Father André was that unusual phenomenon in the eighteenth century, a Jesuit who was also a Cartesian. He had become the latter by way of Malebranche.

Batteux, Abbé Charles, 1713-80. His treatise on aesthetics is entitled *Les Beaux-Arts réduits à un même principe,* Paris, 1746. This little book has a frontispiece the subject of which is Phaedra and Socrates sitting under a plane tree and reading a dissertation on beauty, a subject taken from Plato's *Phaedra.* However, Batteux was not really a Platonist but rather an Aristotelian. He taught Greek and Latin at the Collège Royal, became a member of the Académie des Inscriptions in 1757, and was elected to the Académie Française in 1765. His treatise on the fine arts is delightful reading: it is all so simple and it dissolves, one would say today, so many problems. The only one he leaves us with was pointed to by Diderot. Just what does the imitation of *la belle nature* mean? But of course the point is that this is not properly a philosophical but an artistic problem. You do not answer this by way of discussion, proofs, and logical arguments, but simply by artistic production. As for Batteux's reduction, it is simply this: ". . . que le Génie, qui est le père des arts, doit imiter la nature. Secondement, qu'il ne doit point l'imiter telle qu'elle est. Troisièmement, que le goût pour qui les arts sont faits, et qui en est le juge, doit être satisfait quand la nature est bien choisie et bien imité par les arts." This was said by Kant later, but with greater strain for the reader. There is no question of *rules* here. It is all ex post facto reasoning, is based on Aristotle and Horace, and is sufficiently vague to leave the poet and painter to his devices. Batteux, in contradistinction to the German aestheticians who used and abused him, never talks of the arts as if they were emanations of an absolute Beauty of the Godhead, but knows and says the arts were made by man for men and sees them and treats them in terms of conventions, fictions, and agreeable illusions.

5. "Discours sur la Nature de l'Eglogue," in *Oeuvres*, Paris, 1818, III, 51. Fontenelle (1657-1757) is not mentioned in the still standard *History of Esthetics* by Gilbert and Kuhn; Bayer mentions him in a footnote in a discussion of Hume, who read Fontenelle. Yet his role in the battle between the Ancients and Moderns, his considerations on literature and the theatre, rules and poetry, his understanding that all these artistic manifestations were tied to social forces and history make him a founder of a novel type of criticism. Furthermore, his manner of resolving certain questions, his approach to the muddle of the Ancients and Moderns, is reminiscent of the present-day analytical philosophy practiced in Britain. For his role in the Enlightenment see Herbert Butterfield, *The Origins of Modern Science*, London, 1950.

6. Corneille's *Discours sur le poème dramatique*, from which this quotation is taken, may be found in various editions of his works. For more on the rules see the important study of René Bray, *La Formation de la Doctrine Classique en France*, Paris, 1927.

7. Boileau, *Satire IX*; the second quotation is from the *Art poétique*.

8. In *Oeuvres*, Pléiade edition, I, 1301.

9. For a discussion of the academic doctrines see André Fontaine, *Les Doctrines d'Art en France, de Poussin à Diderot*,

Paris, 1909; for a slightly different view and approach, the short discussion in the *Histoire générale de l'art*, Paris, 1938, III, 342-47. The author of these pages of this collective work holds that academicism in the seventeenth century was mostly verbal, but that in the course of the eighteenth century, due to the influence of antiquarians like Caylus, it became a fact. In the seventeenth century one talked one way and one painted another, while collecting and buying irrespective of the discourses pronounced in the Academy. A perusal of eighteenth century catalogues will verify this. An excellent instance of it would be the Marquis de Marigny, who, in his capacity as Minister of Works, fostered and encouraged history painting and the grand manner, but who privately had a marked predilection for the *petite manière*.

10. Félibien, *Entretiens sur la vie et les ouvrages de Nicolas Poussin*, Geneva, 1957, p. 91 (reprint).

11. The opening lines of this chapter are not to be construed as implying that science "caused" a new type of criticism. The entire question of the relation between art and science in the seventeenth century is a very complicated one which we cannot treat here. We shall here merely ask the reader to keep in mind that science changes as much as art, as well as do the attitudes to both. Further, in the seventeenth century amateurs of letters and arts might also have been amateurs of science at the same time, so that both the arts and the search for knowledge were often practiced as a disinterested activity. As one writer in the *Mercure Galant* wrote concerning Fontenelle's knowledge and understanding of science, "Il n'aime les belles connaissances que pour s'en servir en honnête homme." The expression *belles connaissances* is quite revealing: the sciences, like some of the fine arts, could thus also be considered the ornaments of the mind, to use an eighteenth century phrase.

12. For more on the intellectual background of the period, see J. S. Spink, *French Free-Thought from Gassendi to Voltaire*, London, 1960; R.H. Popkin, *The History of Scepticism from Erasmus to Descartes*, Assen & N.Y., 1964; Herbert Butterfield, *op. cit.* For a short and lucid account of the *Querelle* see Philippe Van Tieghem, *Petite Histoire des Grandes Doctrines Littéraires en France*, Paris, P.U.F.; 1954.

13. On Montesquieu see Robert Shackleton, *Montesquieu, A Critical Biography*, Oxford Univ. Press, 1962; and for a résumé of his views on aesthetical matters see the last chapter of Paul Barrière's *Un Grand Provincial: Charles de Secondat*, Bordeaux and Paris, 1946. Montesquieu's various writings are readily available in the Pléiade edition of his works.

14. *Lettre écrite à l'Académie Française* (1753 edition), p. 307.

15. Condillac, *Oeuvres complètes*, Paris, 1821, V, 485-86.

16. In *Mélanges de littérature, d'histoire et de philosophie*, Berlin, 1753.

17. Function and ornament were not thought antithetical in the seventeenth or eighteenth century (or before) and their relation to each other was put quite well by Father Bouhours, a seventeenth century critic, in his *De la Manière de bien penser dans les ouvrages de l'esprit*: "Nous l'avons dit, et on ne saurait trop le redire: la vérité est à la pensée ce que les fondements sont aux édifices: elle la soutient et la rend solide. Mais une bâtiment qui ne serait que solide, n'aurait pas de quoi plaire à ceux qui se connaissent en architecture. Outre la solidité, on veut de la grandeur, de l'agrément, et même de la délicatesse dans les maisons bien bâties."

18. Voltaire, "Essai sur la poésie épique," in *Oeuvres*, ed. Moland, VIII, 319. For more on the relation of the aesthetic judgment and time, see J. Claude Piguet, "Temps et Eternité" in *Revue Philosophique de la France et de l'Etranger*, 1961, nos. 1-2, 247-61.

19. Du Bos, *Réflexions critiques sur la poésie et sur la peinture*, La Haye, 1732, II, 291. All quotations are from this edition. Du Bos' aesthetics has been thoroughly discussed by Eugen Teubner in "Die Kunstphilosophie des Abbé Du Bos" in *Zeitschrift für Aesthetik und Allgemeine Kunstwissenschaft*, XVII, no. 4, 61 ff.

20. Charles Rollin, "Réflexions générales sur le goût" in his often edited *De la Manière d'enseigner et d'étudier les Belles Lettres par rapport à l'esprit et au coeur*, Paris, 1754, I, ciiij.

21. On the literary and social salons, see Marguerite Glotz and Madeleine Maire, *Les Salons du XVIIIe Siècle*, Paris, 1948; also

the *Mémoires* of Marmontel in *Oeuvres posthumes*, Paris, 1804, Vol. II. For the rivalry between men of letters and artists see the essay by J. Seznec, "Falconet, Voltaire et Diderot" in *Studies on Voltaire and the Eighteenth Century*, II, 43-54.

22. Quoted from Francis Henry Taylor, *The Taste of Angels*, Boston, 1948, p. 364.

23. On Caylus see S. Rocheblave, *Essai sur le Comte de Caylus*, Paris, 1889; for some of his writings, *Vies d'Artistes au XVIIIe Siècle*, ed. by A. Fontaine, Paris, 1910.

24. On collecting in the eighteenth century, see Taylor, *op. cit.*, book VII for France, book VIII for England.

25. Shaftesbury, "Advice to an Author" in *Characteristics*, 1711, II, 322. Shaftesbury is often treated as an aesthetician. He occupies important chapters in Bayer, and in Gilbert and Kuhn. While it is true that he wrote on the arts, beauty, taste, and genius, so did most of his contemporaries. Upon reading him I rather thought of him as a *moraliste* who has more in common with La Rochefoucauld or La Bruyère than he does with professional philosophers like Kant. Shaftesbury was, it seems to me, concerned with the art of being a man. See the excellent and concise study by R. L. Brett, *The Third Earl of Shaftesbury*, London, 1951.

26. Henry Home, Lord Kames, *The Elements of Criticism*, Edinburgh, 1769, II, pp. 497, 498. Voltaire gave this work a stinging review in the *Gazette littéraire* of Lausanne when the book first appeared in 1764. His impatience with Home's approach marks well enough one of the differences between the French and Scottish approach to the question, or, national traits aside, between an artistic and "scientific" approach. To Voltaire, Home's work was merely an example of useless metaphysics and a lengthy exercursion into the obvious.

27. Charles Picard, "Pour l'étude d'une 'renaissance' méconnue: Propos sur l'Art Hellenistique (323-31 A.J.C.)," in *Revue philosophique de la France et de l'Etranger*, 1961, Avril-Sept., 141-49.

28. See the essay by Walter J. Ong, S.J., "The Vernacular Matrix of the New Criticism" in *The Barbarian Within*, N.Y., 1962, pp. 177-205.

29. G. Wildenstein, "Talma et les peintres," *Gazette des Beaux-Arts*, 1960, pp. 169-76; also the writings of Diderot on the theater and especially his concern for mime, in *Oeuvres esthétiques*, pp. 189-287.

30. This discussion of the language of painting is in large part based on Ferdinand Brunot's treatment of it in his *Histoire de la langue française des origines à 1900*, Vol. VI, section iii *passim*.

31. This "digression" written in the early eighteenth century, is reprinted in his *Oeuvres complètes*, Paris, 1781, IX, pp. 556-66. The whole point of the essay is that beauty and the *je ne sais quoi* are rarely found together. The tale concerns a man who wanders into two gardens, one housing Beauty, the other the *je ne sais quoi*. The first garden is described as grand, magnificent, superb, and of exact symmetry. That of the *je ne sais quoi*, however, seemed to be the work of happy chance; all seemed in disorder, though in the best of taste, and created a charming effect whose reason or cause could not be found or fixed. Beauty, in short, could be defined; the *je ne sais quoi* could not. The entire essay is an excellent illustration of the contrast between the *Grand Goût* and what we have come to call the rococo.

32. This idea was stated by Du Bos, who thought the best judges of a painting were not the professionals, but men of taste. However, in the course of the eighteenth century it took on different forms, some of which were rather ludicrous. The Swiss painter Liotard, for example, thought that the closer a person was to nature, the less educated and therefore the more free of prejudices, the better a judge of portraits he or she might be. This was to overlook the essential difference between art and nature.

33. *Salons*, ed. Jean Seznec and Jean Adhémar, Oxford Univ. Press, II, 57.

34. On the neoclassic and the past, see John Summerson, *Architecture in Britain, 1530-1830* (The Pelican History of Art), p. 247: "Neo-Classicism" is here used to describe that new spirit which, about the middle of the eighteenth century, altered the balance of the European's attitude to the past and therefore to

the present and future." See also the excellent work of Louis Hautecoeur, *Histoire de l'architecture classique en France*, Paris, Picard, 1952, Vol. IV, especially pp. 16-69. A more intellectual approach is given by Pierre Francastel in his chapter on "Le Néo-Classique" in the Larousse series *L'Art et l'Homme*, edited by René Huyghe, Vol. III:

> Quand on parle de retour à l'Antique, on replace habituellement le XVIIIᵉ dans le cycle de la Renaissance. Il est grand temps de l'explorer comme un siècle révolutionnaire. Il n'est pas seulement le siècle des Académies, il est celui de l'histoire. Ce ne sont pas les boudoirs et la technique du Beau qui le laissent vivant; c'est sa découverte de l'historicité, qui n'implique pas un retour aux normes de la pureté, mais une vue différen-tielle de l'histoire. (268)

While it may be possible for us to see certain aspects of eighteenth century thought as revolutionary, it may also be stressed that the implications of such thought often escaped the thinkers. It is extremely important to limit the meaning of the words used by the men of the past. A legitimate question is whether, despite this awareness of the past, the eighteenth century really discovered historical thinking as this has come to be construed since the end of the nineteenth century and German historicism. On the whole the neoclassic, while inspired by the past and made possible by a better knowledge of it, was also in a certain sense an attempt to escape history. Return to the past implies less a sense of historical movement than the hope that somehow time may be countered.

35. On the number of eighteenth centuries see Roland Mortier's essay, "Unité ou scission du siècle des lumières?" in the Transactions of the First International Congress on the Enlightenment, *Studies on Voltaire and the Eighteenth Century*, Vol. XXVI, 1963, 1207-21; also, in the same series, Janine Buenzod, "De l'*Aufklärung* au *Sturm und Drang*: continuité ou rupture?", XXIV, 1963, pp. 289-313; for a discussion of the English Enlightenment, Robert Voitle, "The Reason of the English Enlightenment," XXVII, 1963, pp. 1735-74.

36. In his important *Réflexions sur l'imitation des artistes grecs dans la peinture et dans la sculpture*, first published in German in 1755, Winckelmann wrote: "La température d'une atmosphère douce, pure et sereine, avait sans doute une grande influence sur la constitution physique des grecs; et les exercises mâles auxquels ils étaient accountumés dans leur jeunesse, achevaient de leur donner une forme noble et élégante." Quoted from the *Recueil de différentes pièces sur les arts*, trans. Huber, Paris, 1785, p. 5. It is interesting to note how different this attitude is from that of Fontenelle, who in the late seventeenth century posed this same question of climatic influence: he shows much more skepticism than the enthusiastic Winckelmann. Fontenelle was inclined to put more stress on human institutions and history in order to explain differences between ancients and moderns. But by the end of the century the Greeks were thought of much as was the noble savage; the savages drawn for the illustrations of the voyages of Cook or Bougainville looked remarkably Greek.

37. The moral revival was given exemplary form by the personal action and life of Rousseau, Citizen of Geneva. When Rousseau found success in letters he reformed himself and first began this reform through that of his dress: "Je commençai ma reforme par ma parure; je quittai la dorure et les bas blancs, je pris une perruque ronde, je posai l'épée, je vendis ma montre, en me disant avec une joie incroyable: Grâce au ciel je n'aurai plus besoin de savoir l'heure qu'il est." This was his way of quitting the rococo style insofar as dress was concerned. It is noteworthy too that by a reform of 1775 for the students of the Academy in Rome, the students were enjoined to be sober, simple, and virtuous in their dress as well as their person. The call for virtue, however, goes back some time before this date. Rousseau's *First Discourse* dates from 1749. Montesquieu's *Esprit des lois*, in which virtue is equated with the republican form of government, dates from 1748.

38. For the satire directed against the rococo stlye in architecture and ornament, see Cochin's *Receuil de quelques pièces concernant les arts*, Paris, 1757; these pieces were published in the then influential *Mercure de France*. In the sixties Diderot was one

of the writers who called for virtue among artists and for moral paintings. This call can be traced to the first writings prompted by the Salons; it first took the form of a demand for a return to great painting, to history, and a critique of the current style, or frivolity. The painters of the mid-eighteenth century were unfavorably compared to those of the *Grand Siècle*; only later on did one turn to the Greeks for inspiration.

39. On Laugier see the section devoted to him by Hautecoeur, *op. cit.* in note 34, pp. 54 ff.

40. These appeared throughout this period: 1743, *Prima parte di architettura*; 1748, *Antichità Romane*; 1750, *Carceri*; 1761, *Della magnificenza ed architettura de Romani*; 1765, *Parere su l'architettura.*

41. E.g.: "Le goût du public contribua beaucoup à la décadence de l'art; on accueillit avec transport ces productions brillantes et ephémères; l'appas du gain, la facilité de l'exécution entraina tous les Artistes. Le goût du dessin et de l'antique fut décrié, l'attachement aux principes regardé comme servitude." In *Discours sur l'Origine, le Progrès et l'Etat actuel de la Peinture en France, Contenant des Notices sur les principaux Artistes de l'Académie; pour servir d'introduction au Salon,* Paris, 1785, p. 8. This is an anonymous pamphlet.

42. On this see Nikolaus Pevsner, *Academies of Art Past and Present,* Cambridge Univ. Press, 1940, especially Chap. 4.

43. Quoted by Hautecoeur, *op. cit.* in note 34, IV, 54.

44. Boulton, "Introduction" to Burke's *A Philosophical Enquiry into the Origin of our Ideas of the Sublime and the Beautiful,* London and New York, 1958, p. xxxvi. The Introduction to this new edition, by J. T. Boulton, is itself an excellent and succinct account of British aesthetics in the eighteenth century.

45. For example, Home writes as follows concerning a seventeenth century French critic: "Bossu, a celebrated French critic, gives many rules; but he can discover no better foundation for any of them, than the practice merely of Homer and Virgil, supported by the authority of Aristotle. Strange! that in so long a work, he should never have stumbled upon the question, whether, and how far, do these rules agree with human nature." The point

was, of course, that art had little to do with human nature, likes or dislikes, but with artistic practice and ideal forms. Considerations of what would most benefit or conform to human nature did not enter into it at all. Both the seventeenth century pedants and the eighteenth century empiricists believed in rules, the first in those of art, the latter in rules founded in nature.

46. S. H. Monk, *The Sublime: A Study in Critical Theories in XVIIIth Century England*, N.Y., 1935, p. 236.

Translations of French Passages in the Text

Page 7:

The eclogues preceded the reflections: I composed and then I thought, and to the shame of reason this is what happens most often. Thus I should not be surprised if it were found that I did not follow my own rules; I did not know these well when I was writing: furthermore, it is easier to make rules than to follow them, and it is established by usage that the former does not oblige to the latter.

Page 8:

One must know what these rules are, but it is our misfortune that Aristotle, and later Horace, wrote of them in such a recondite manner as to need interpreters and that those who have wished to serve this purpose have explained these rules as grammarians or philosophers. Since they had more erudition and speculative knowledge than experience of the stage, reading them may make us more learned, but it can hardly give us much light wherewith to succeed [on the stage].

Page 10:

If works written according to the rules do not please, and those not done according to the rules do, it follows that the rules were ill conceived. Let us therefore forget this chicanery whereby they [the pedants] hope to dictate the public's taste and let us, in a comedy, merely consider its effect on us. Let us allow ourselves to be moved in good faith and not reason ourselves out of pleasure.

Pages 12-13:

As we say poetic beauty we ought also to say geometric beauty and medicinal beauty; but we do not: and the reason for it is that we know very well what the object of geometry is, to wit that it consists in proofs; and what the object of medicine is, namely healing; but we don't quite know what agreeableness, the object of poetry, is. We do not know what the natural model to be imitated really is.

Pages 15-16:

Truth was not to the taste of the early centuries of mankind: a useful lie, a happy error, made for the interest of imposters, and the pleasure of the credulous. It was the secret of the great and the wise for governing peoples and the simple in soul.

The genius of our century is totally opposed to this spirit of fables and false mysteries. We love declared truths: good sense prevails over the illusions of fantasy: only solidity and reason content us today. Add to this change of taste, that of knowledge. We envisage nature in a manner different from that of the ancients. The heavens, eternal dwelling place of so many divinities, are now but an immense and fluid space. The same sun still illuminates us, but we give it another course: instead of bedding in the sea, it goes forth to light up another world. The earth, once immobile in the opinion of men, now revolves in that same opinion and with a speed unequaled. All is changed; the gods, nature, politics, mores, taste, manners. Will not such changes also produce some in our works?

Page 21:

Eloquence and poetry require only a certain number of rather limited views (or ideas) as contrasted with the other arts, and these depend principally on the vivacity of the imagination. Now men may have acquired a limited number of such ideas in a short period; and vivacity of imagination requires neither a long series of experiments nor a great number of rules to gain all the perfection it is capable of attaining. But physics, medicine, and mathematics are composed of an infinite number of ideas and depend on exactness of reasoning, which perfects itself extremely slowly, but continuously; sometimes these sciences must be helped by chance experiments which are not always brought to the desired point. It is evident there is no end to this and that the last physicists and mathematicians must naturally be the best.

Pages 23-24:

Homer's *Iliad*, which many know by its reputation rather than from the original, seemed to me to deserve to be put into French verse, in order to amuse the curiosity of those not acquainted with the original language. To this end I interrogated Homer; that is, I read him with attention; and, persuaded while reading him that nothing is perfect and that errors are inseparable from humanity, I guarded myself from prejudices in order not to confuse beauties and errors. And so it seemed to me that the gods and heroes of the Greek poem would not be to our taste; that many episodes would appear too long, that the harangues of the combatants would not be judged strictly necessary, and that the shield of Achilles must strike us as rather confused and unreasonably marvellous. The more I thought upon this, the more I was convinced, and having thought about it for as long as respect to the public required, I decided to change, cut and if need be invent and do what I imagined Homer should have done had he lived in our time.

Page 27:

But what finally suceeds in making us lose the sense of the sublime, prevents us from striking and being struck [by images], is the new philosophy which speaks but of general laws and removes from our mind all particularized notions of the divinity. Reducing everything to the communication of motion it speaks to us but of pure understanding [or mind] clear ideas, reason, principles, consequences. This philosophy, which has descended even to the fair sex, diminishes the taste which we naturally have for poetry.

Page 28:

I read a tempest described in very fine verses: nothing is missing of what could have been seen or felt by those who experienced it; only Neptune raging with his trident was not there. In good faith, shall I regret this, or shall I be wrong not to? What could he have added to what I have seen? I defy him to have raised the waters higher than they were or to have spread more horror in that unfortunate vessel, and so on; reality alone sufficed for all possibilities.

Pages 32-33:

There is no doubt that philosophy has today acquired new degrees of perfection. Thence a certain light not restricted to the area of philosophy, but gaining everywhere, and even reaching the field of letters. Order, clarity, justness of reasoning, which formerely were none too common even among the better authors, are today much more so even among the average writers. This change, which to a certain degree is for the better, is felt almost everywhere. Is poetry to pride itself on the glorious privilege of being exempt from it?

Pages 34-35:

Once clarity and precision are the characteristics of a language, it is no longer possible to write well without also being clear and precise. Even poets must submit to this law if they wish to achieve durable successes. They would be wrong to fall back on their enthusiasm or reputation. Only exactness of expression may accredit those turns of phrase which they are allowed, and in this respect French poetry is most scrupulous.

Page 49:

If real and true passions procure the soul its most acute sensations only at the price of ill effects, and since the happy moments they make us live are followed by days of sadness, could not art manage to separate the ill effects of most passions from what is most agreeable in them? Could not art, so to say, fashion creatures of a new nature? Could it not produce objects capable of exciting passions within us the moment we feel them, but incapable of causing real harm and true afflictions afterwards? Poetry and painting have succeeded in this.

Page 66:

Far from judging a piece we hear for the first time, we distrust its beauties as long as it is in the mouths of the actors; and however affected we were by it, we suspend our judgment until we have read it; and quite truly, it does not always give us the same pleasure on paper as it did on the stage.

Thus we scrupulously examine a poem, he went on, before giving it our esteem; the reputation of its author, no matter how great it may be, cannot dazzle us. Even when Lope de Vega and Calderón produced new works, they found severe judges among their admirers, who raised them to the height of glory only after having judged them worthy of it.

Page 67:

Since the primary object of poetry and painting is to move us, poems and paintings are good insofar as they succeed in moving and drawing us to them. A work which touches us a great deal must on the whole be excellent. For the same reason, a work which neither touches nor attracts us, is worthless, and if criticism finds no infringements of the rules in such a work, it is because a work may be bad even though there be no mistakes, while one filled with infringements of the rules may be excellent.

Page 68:

All artists read with profit his [Du Bos'] *Reflections on poetry, painting and music.* It is the most useful book on these matters which has ever been written in any of the European nations.

What makes it a good work is that there are few errors and many true, new, and profound thoughts. It is not a methodical book; but the author thinks and makes us think. Yet he knew no music, was never capable of writing verses, and possessed not a single painting; but he had read, seen, heard, and thought much.

Page 69:

Sentiment is a far better guide to whether a work touches us, and makes the impression it is supposed to make, than all the dissertations composed by critics to explicate its merit and calculate its perfections and faults. The means of discussion and analysis which these gentlemen use is in truth good enough if you wish to know why a work does or does not please, but it is not as good as sentiment for deciding the question itself. Does the work please, or does it not? Is the work in general good or bad? It is the same thing. Reasoning thus must intervene in the general judgment we give a poem or a painting only to explain a decision of sentiment, explain which faults prevent its being pleasing, and which are the agreeable parts which make it attractive.

Page 72:

If an entire nation was in the early development of the fine arts united in the love of authors filled with faults and in time despised, it was because such authors possessed natural beauties felt by everyone and because no one was yet in a position to unravel their imperfections. Thus was Lucilius beloved of the Romans because Virgil made them forget him, and Régnier appreciated by the French before Boileau appeared.

Page 75:

All times have produced heroes and politicians; all peoples have gone through revolutions: all histories are almost the same for those who would but fill their memories with facts. But whoever thinks, and what is more rare, whoever has taste, knows only four centuries in the history of the world.

Page 79:

It is almost impossible to make good new tragedies because most of the good plots were taken by the first authors. For us it is an exhausted mine. There will come a people which in regard to us will be what we are to the Greeks and Romans. A new language, new mores, new circumstances, will make a new body of tragedies. Their authors will take from nature what we have already taken from her, or from our own authors, and soon they will be as exhausted as we are.

Pages 81-82:

I therefore conclude, using the words of Tacitus, that the world is subject to changes and vicissitudes whose periodicity is unknown to us, but those revolutions successively bring back manners and barbarism, the talents of the mind and the power of the body, and consequently the progress of the arts and sciences, their languor and their decline.

Pages 83-84:

Again, what is most striking in this illustrious century is that despite the wars excited by ambition, and in spite of the troubles of religion which began to shake nations, this same genius made the arts flourish in Rome, Naples, Florence, Venice, Ferrara, and from there carried its light into Europe, softening men in almost all the provinces of Christian Europe.

Pages 86-87:

My first reflection is that there are nations and times where letters and the arts do not flourish, even though the moral causes work actively for their advancement.

The second reflection is that arts and letters do not attain perfection by a long and slow progress proportional to the time given their cultivation, but rather by a sudden progress [or leap]. . . .

Finally, great painters were always the contemporaries of

great poets and both lived at the same time as their greatest contemporaries. At such times a spirit of perfection spread over the entire human race in their nations.

Page 89:

Noticeably, men born in Europe and its neighboring coasts have always been more adept than other peoples in the arts, the sciences, and political government. Everywhere Europeans have carried their arms, they have subjugated the natives of the country. The Europeans have always beaten then even when they were ten against thirty. Often the Europeans defeated them even though they were but ten to a hundred.

Page 101:

It is, in painting, knowledge of the most beautiful products of nature and those most befitting this art. There are several painters who have known how to imitate nature perfectly in their works but have made a bad *choice*. This *choice* must be in the taste and manner of the Ancients, that is, in the taste of those magnificent works, of the Greeks as well as the Romans, which have been preserved.

Page 103:

I allowed the impression time to come and enter. I opened my soul to its effects. I allowed myself to be penetrated by them . . . I learned what is meant by fine drawing and truth to nature. I understood the magic of color and shadow. I knew color. I acquired a feeling for flesh tones. Alone, I have meditated what I saw and heard; and these terms of the art, unity, variety, contrast, symmetry, ordering of the parts, composition, characters, expression, so familiar on my tongue, so vague in my mind, circumscribed and fixed themselves.

Pages 126-127:

Speculations upon the nature of the rules do not give genius to those who possess it not, they do not much help those who have it, and most often even people of genius cannot be helped by these speculations. What, then, are they good for? They allow those who love reasoning to analyze the original ideas of beauty and to place within the empire of philosophy those things which appear the most independent of it and are believed to be left to the vagaries of taste.

Index

Academicism, 98, 105, 111-15
Academies, 113
Academy, 14, 62, 105, 111, 114
Addison, Joseph, 1, 129, 131
Aesthetics: modern, 1; philosophical, 2, 13, 132; types of, 3, 5; British, 4, 68, 75, 118, 122, 125, 131; French, 4, 68, 122, 131; German, 4, 68, 75, 118, 121, 125, 131; as reflection on art, 5; of doubtful utility, 134
Aesthetics, history of: independent of men, 2; written by philosophers, 3-7; as progress to Kant, 6; as misfortunes of philosophers, 12; in the eighteenth century, 128
Alberti, Leon Battista, 77
Alembert, Jean le Rond d', 36-37
Algarotti, Francesco, 116
Alison, Archibald, 125, 129-31
Amateurs, 47, 53, 59-60, 68, 69, 99, 118
Ancients. See Ancients and Moderns
Ancients and Moderns, Quarrel of: and science, 15-16; general discussion of, 16-25; questions implied in it, 16; ancients the young, 18; ancients not superior to moderns, 20; mentioned, 44, 86, 105, 117, 123. See also Homer; La Motte-Houdard; Poetry; Science

André, Yves Marie, 3, 4, 68, 127, 136
Angiviller, Comte d', 115
Antique, 38, 101, 107. See also Greeks; Romans
Antiquomanes, 107, 116
Antiquomania, 53
Antwerp, school of, 91
Architecture: Régence, 50; neoclassic, 110, 111-12
Argenville, Dezallier d', 59
Aristotle, 8, 9, 117
Art: and science, 6, 15-16, 38, 78, 90; and truth, 17-18; and imitation, 39, 41, 61, 107, 131; as decor of life, 49-50; and society, 51, 68, 77, 79, 85, 91-92; and civilization, 77, 84, 87-89; and public power, 80, 84-85, 114; and war, 83; and climate, 86; autonomous, 78, 105-06; mentioned, 20, 49, 61. See also Grands Siècles; Neoclassic style; Poetry; Taste
Art criticism, 61, 102
Art critics, 62, 95, 103-04
Artists. See Painters
Arts d'agréments, 119
Audience. See Public, and arts
Augustus, Caesar, 18, 39, 80, 86

Batteux, Charles, 3, 4, 68, 74, 95, 136-37
Baudelaire, Charles, 18, 127

157